Reinvent Yourself

Owner

· ·

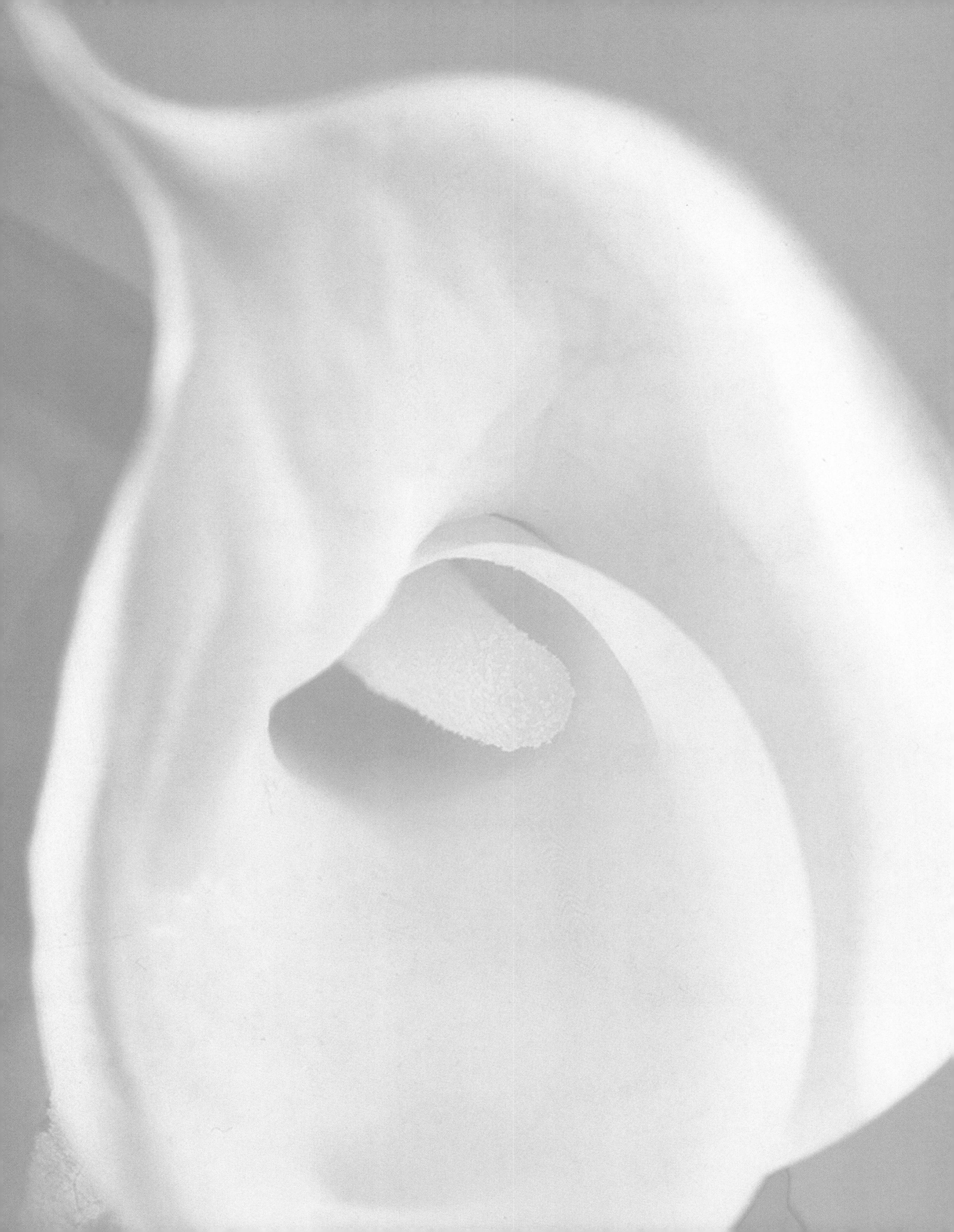

JOURNAL

Reinvent Yourself

Start Your Journey Today of Living Your Best Life

Denise A. Barrow

I'm thankful to God for being my Rock. I'm thankful for my (single-parent) mother, who taught me how to persevere in times of adversity. I'm thankful for my children, who've given me reason to be resilient. Thank you to my best-friend, for your invaluable friendship and support. Thanks to my family, for teaching me the importance of self-sufficiency. Last but not least, I'm thankful for the experiences that I've endured to create the person I am today.

And to my Readers:
Thank you.
My goal is and will always be to enhance the lives of others.
May you be enlightened!

The author has asserted the rights to be identified as the author of this Work in accordance with the Copyright, Designs and Patents Act 1988

Book design by Adam Hay Studio

Printed and bound by BookBaby

ISBN: 978-0-578-88523-0

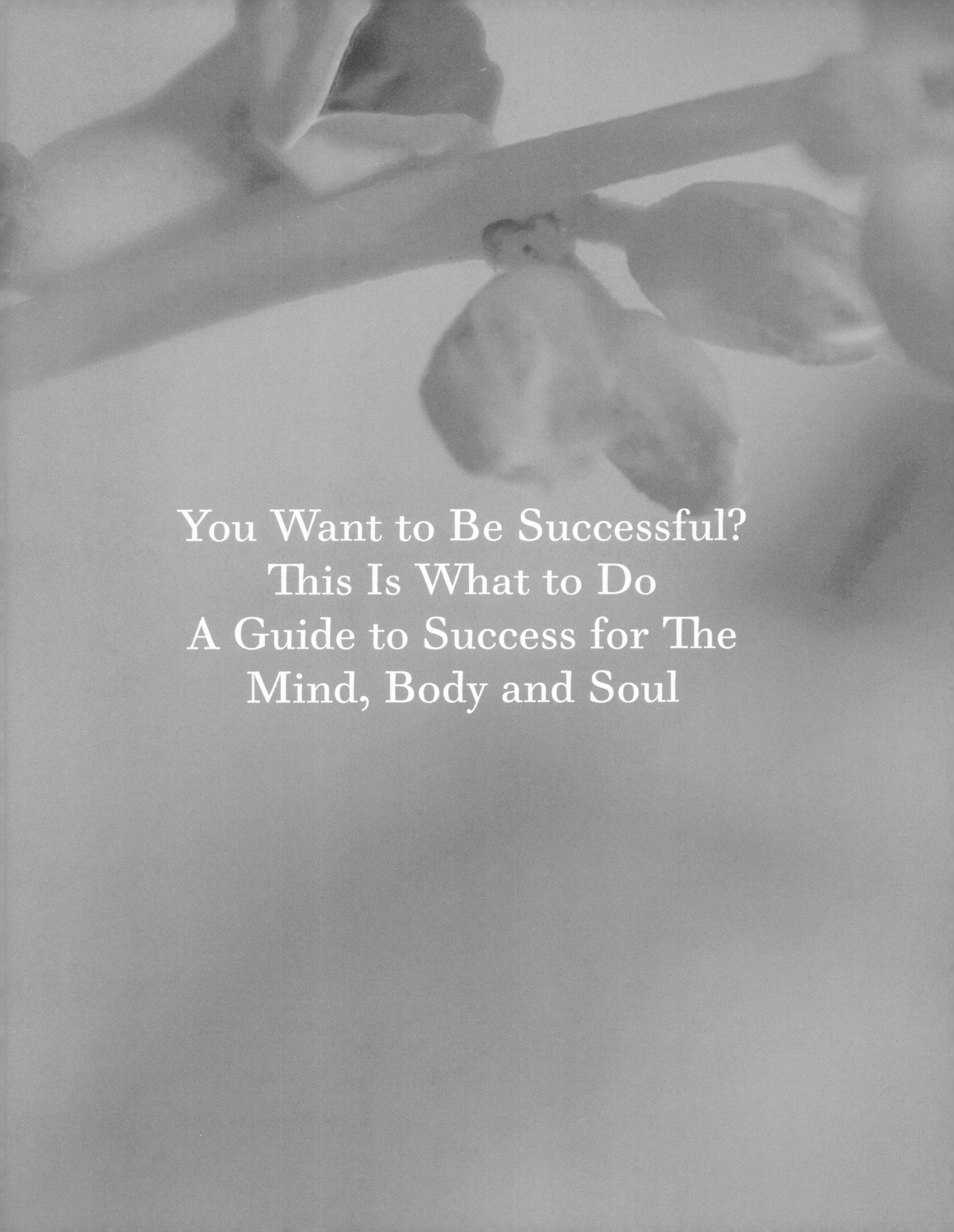

You Want to Be Successful? This Is What to Do A Guide to Success for The Mind, Body and Soul

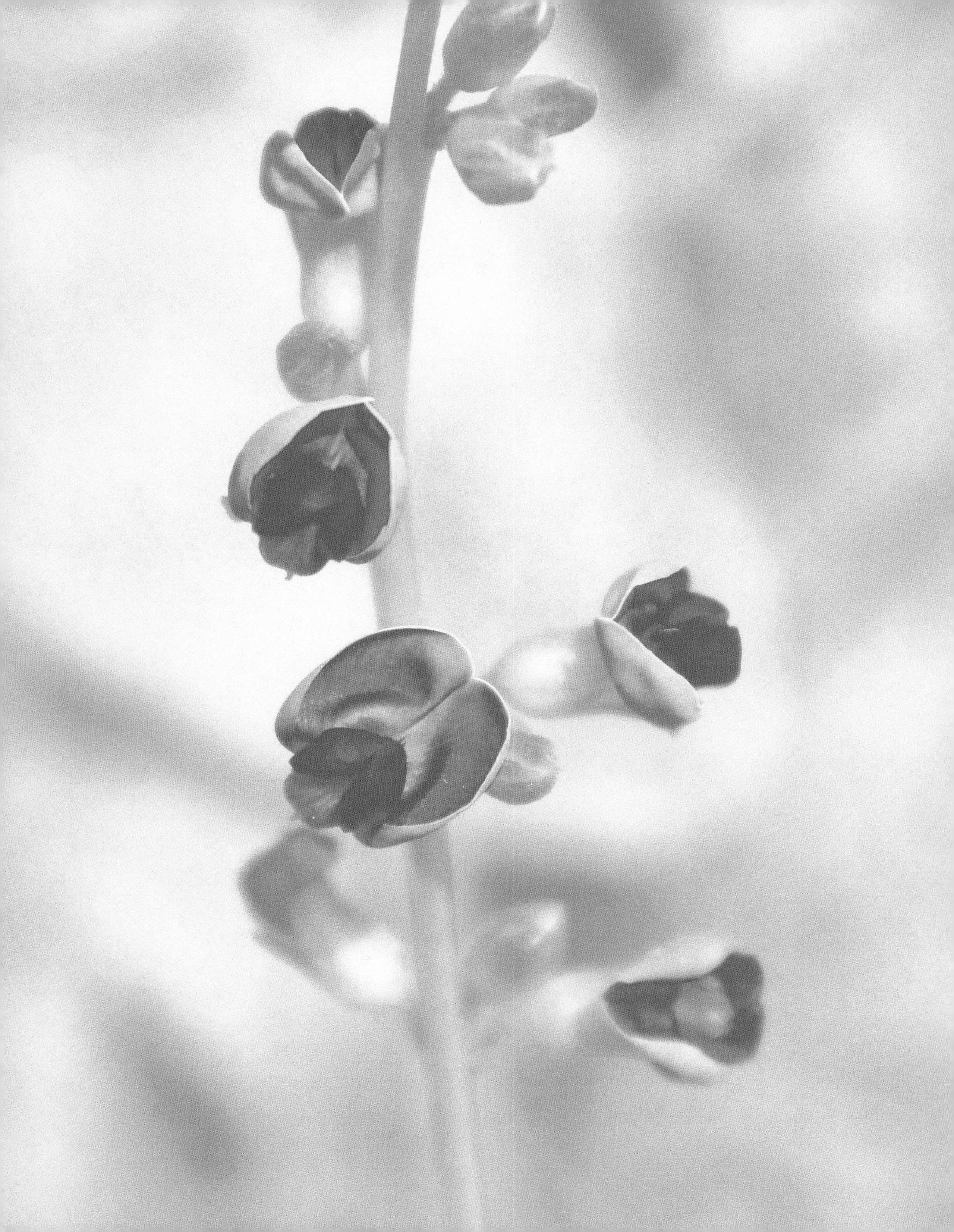

Preface

I am a woman. A woman who's suffered countless traumas and has questioned her worth, value and purpose. A woman who has searched for love in all the wrong places. Just to realize that self-love is first and foremost. I'm the same woman who chose not to let her experiences define her. I've discovered that God has never allowed me to feel comfortable in situations that I don't belong (personally and professionally). I've experienced many adversities. However, I persevered. I've also come to realize that everything in my life has happened for a reason. I hope to write that book one day, but for now, I'll share with you how I did it . . .

For me, God's grace and mercy brought me a long way. I would be nothing without The Heavenly Father. For those of you who don't share my views, please know that this is a judgement-free zone. We all have the right to our own beliefs.

Introspection: a reflective looking inward: an examination of one's own thoughts and feelings. ("Introspection," [Merriam-Webster's Collegiate Dictionary]).

This journal, guide and activity workbook is an easy way to self-enhancement. It will help you gain perspective of yourself and environment. The book is to be used as a tool, which is designed to assist the owner in coming to an understanding about themselves from a holistic point of view. In our efforts to enhance ourselves, we must refrain from myopic perceptions when assessing our lives. Applying comprehensive introspection will increase a healthy self-image which will enhance our overall growth.

This is a great resource for clinicians and their clients, as well as individuals who want to enhance themselves in all areas of their lives. I've always found daily journaling to be rewarding. If you enjoy journaling or have always wanted to journal, you'll love this tool! The activity workbook contains an empowering poem, and a total of fifty positive affirmations and directives. There are four fields to address your thoughts, feelings, behaviors and goals. The best way for you to get the most out of the activities is to be honest with yourself. Read each entry carefully, conduct introspection, put the task in practice then proceed to address the four areas. Also, you should take notes of these topics. You are encouraged to implement all fifty tasks, as they apply to your life. Documentation of dates will help you record and track your progress.

This workbook was made for you. Enjoy your journey!

Enhancing Your Authentic Self

Life is a dream; I'll wake up when I die.

We construct a trajectory of poor choices

And fail to understand why.

God put me in this world, and how do I repay him?

Am I making the best of my life?

Or has my mind become a vessel in which I'm enslaved in?

Thoughts need comprehension.

Comprehension need structure.

Structure need implementation.

You've got to start somewhere.

Why not here? Why not now?

The limitlessness of you, the obligation to whom be your true motivation.

But you've got to do the work.

How much are you willing to put into yourself?

That commitment you give to your 9-5 grind….

Never compensates for your existential wealth.

Stop waiting. Stop putting things off.

Make every breath be a breath of consciousness.

Often times, we know better; so why not do better?

Develop a mastery of mindfulness and not pretentiousness.

Do what you say you're going to do.

Let your word be your bond.

However, you must be present in introspection,

When the mind, body and soul simultaneously fail to respond.

You are sufficient.

Authentic and unique, God created you as bright as a morning star.

We spend so much time trying to be who we're not

Instead, love yourself enough to enhance who you are.

I've got to do better.

I will do better.

I am better.

Those with persistence in finding their purpose will often fulfill their quest to endeavor.

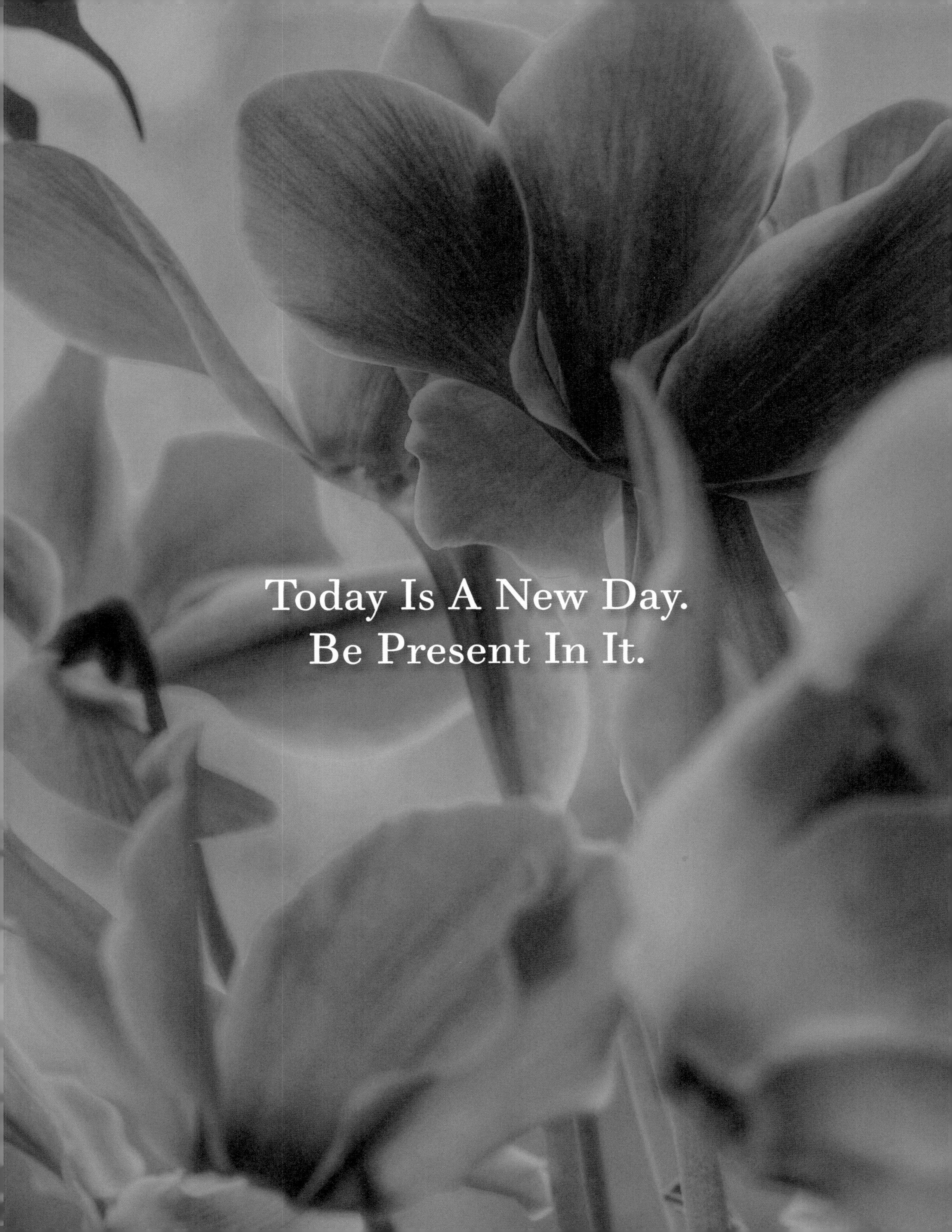
Today Is A New Day.
Be Present In It.

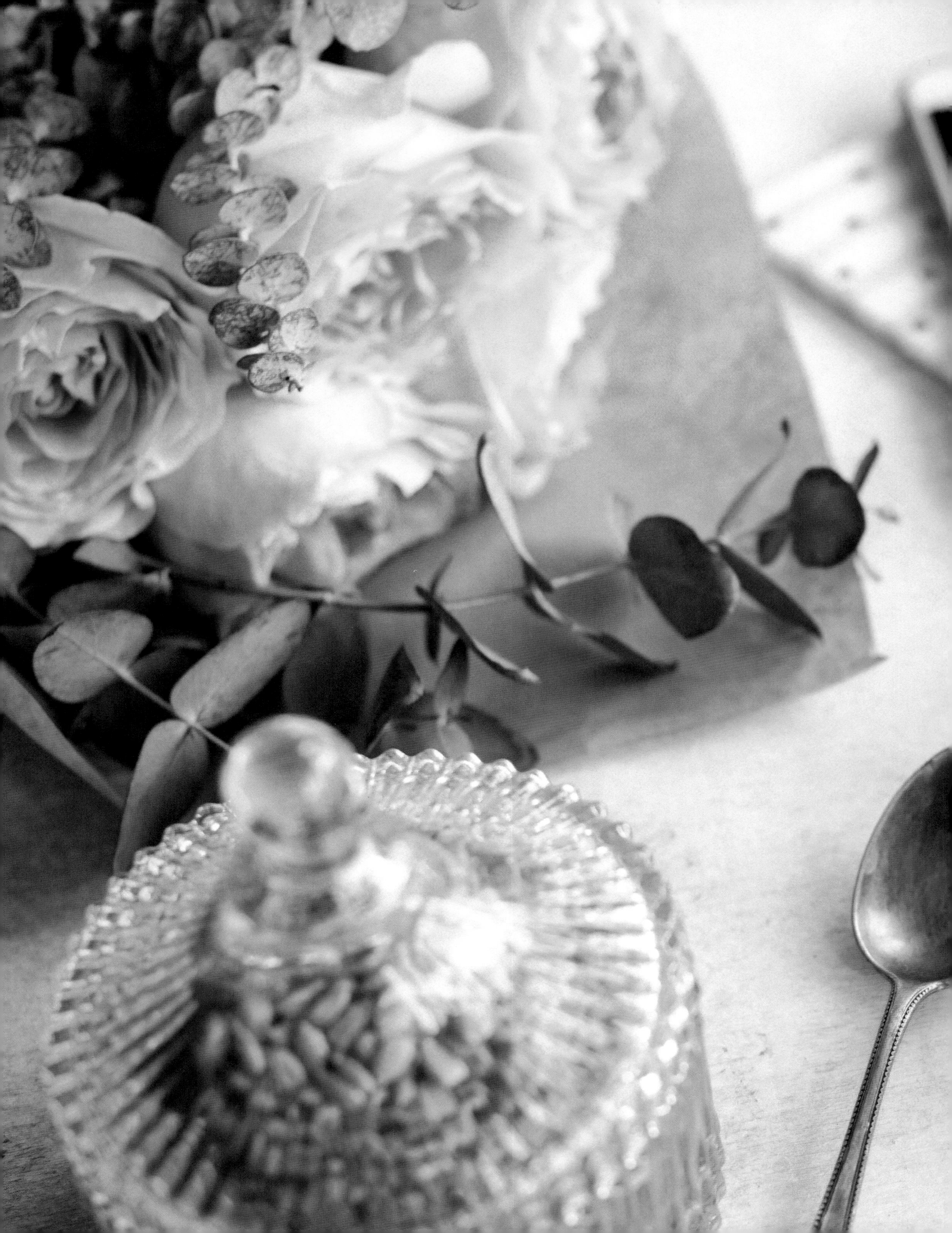

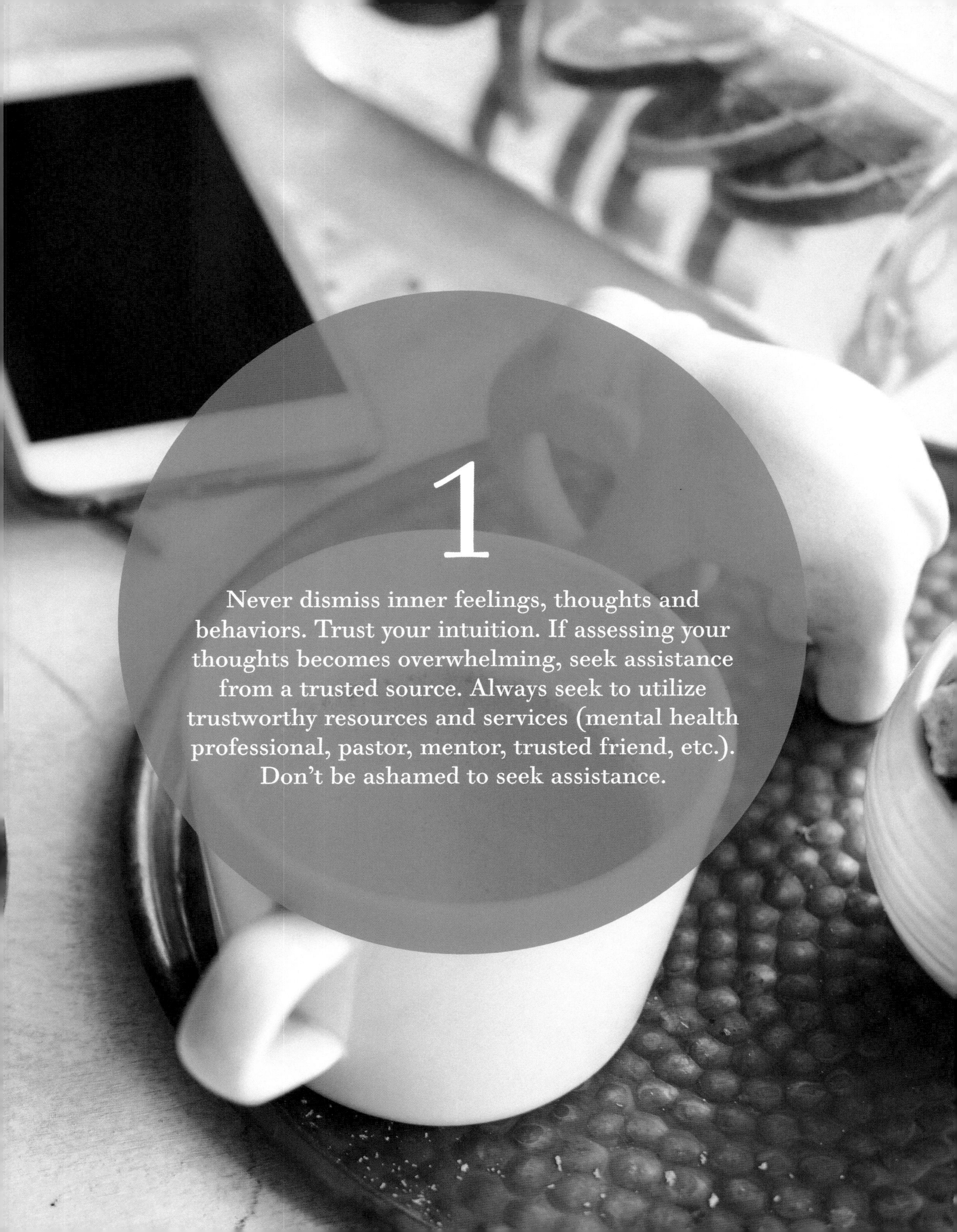

1

Never dismiss inner feelings, thoughts and behaviors. Trust your intuition. If assessing your thoughts becomes overwhelming, seek assistance from a trusted source. Always seek to utilize trustworthy resources and services (mental health professional, pastor, mentor, trusted friend, etc.). Don't be ashamed to seek assistance.

Date
....

Thought/s:
....
....
....
....

Feeling/s:
....
....
....
....

Behavior/s:
....
....
....
....

Goal/s:
....
....
....
....

Date

Notes

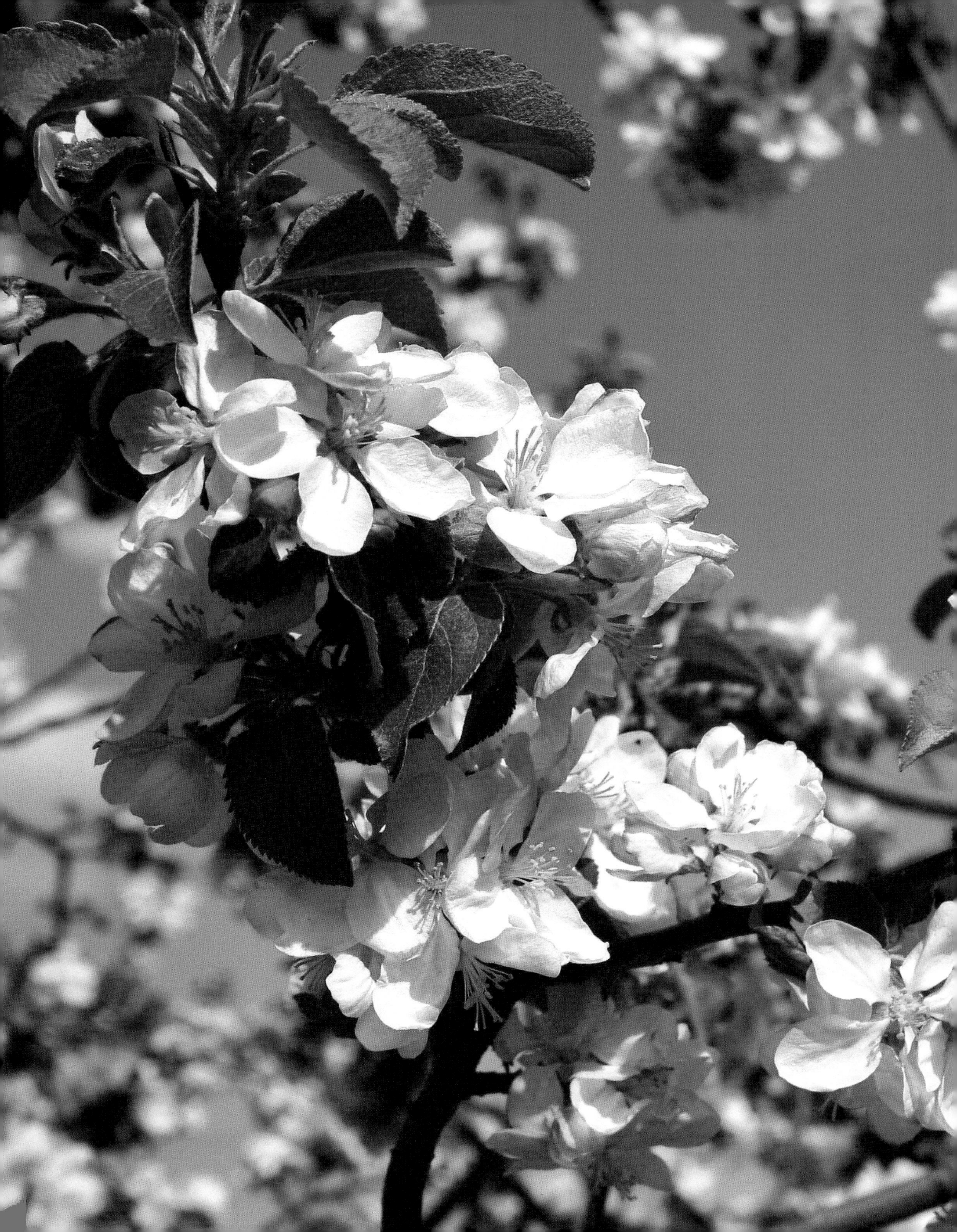

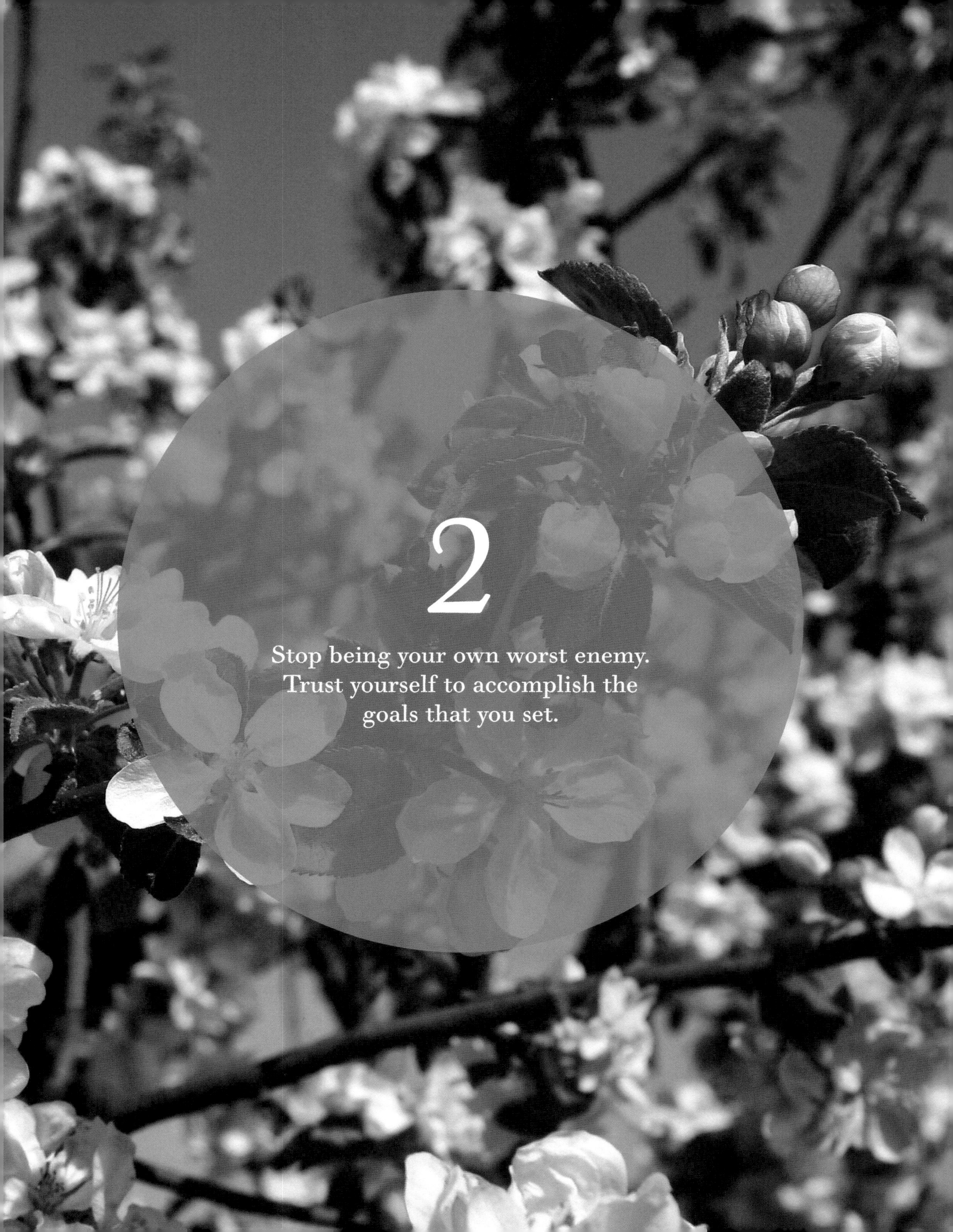

2

Stop being your own worst enemy.
Trust yourself to accomplish the
goals that you set.

Date
....

Thought/s:
....
....
....
....

Feeling/s:
....
....
....
....
....

Behavior/s:
....
....
....
....
....

Goal/s:
....
....
....
....

Date
....

Notes
....

....

....

....

....

....

....

....

....

....

....

....

....

....

....

....

....

....

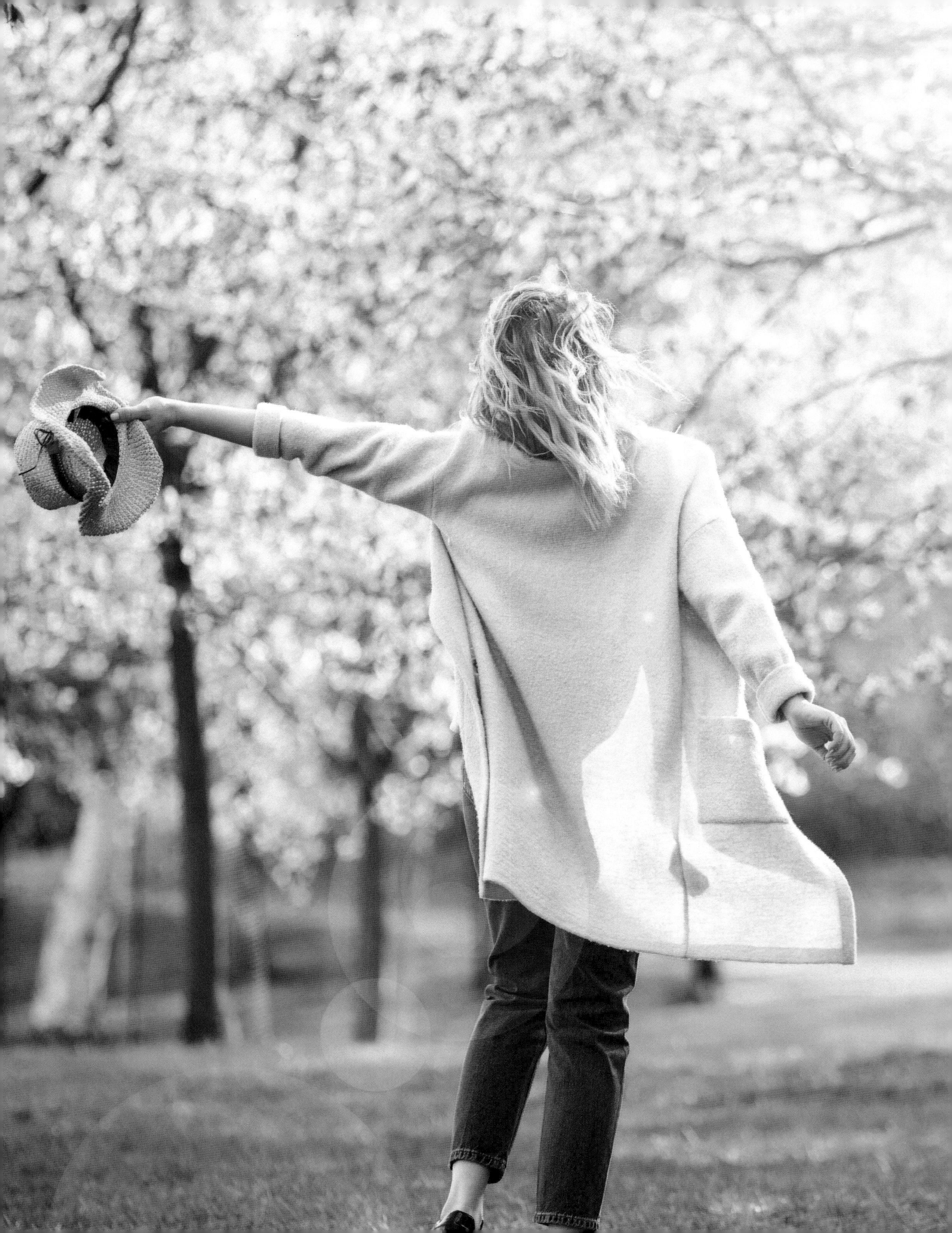

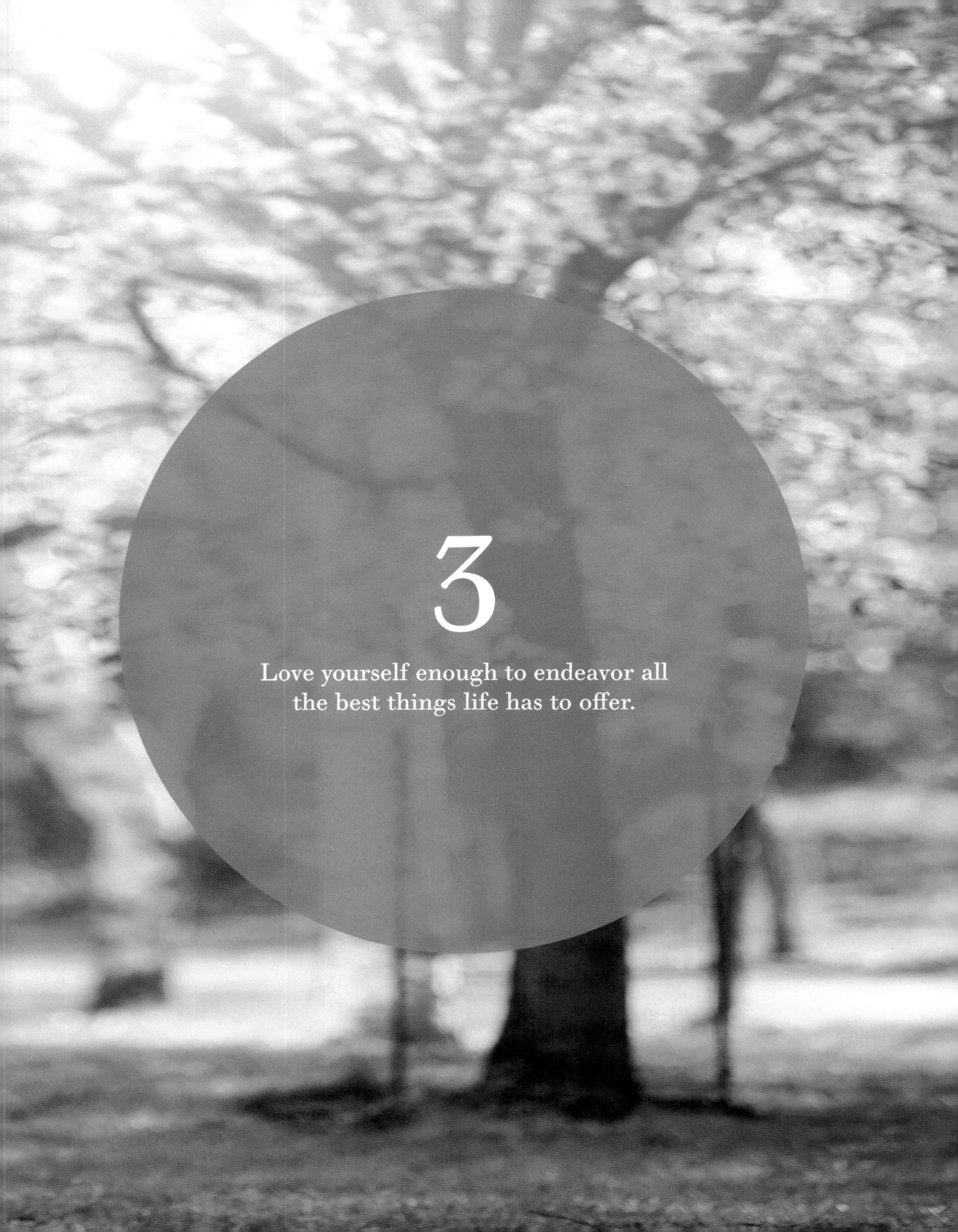

3

Love yourself enough to endeavor all
the best things life has to offer.

Date

Thought/s:

Feeling/s:

Behavior/s:

Goal/s:

Date

Notes

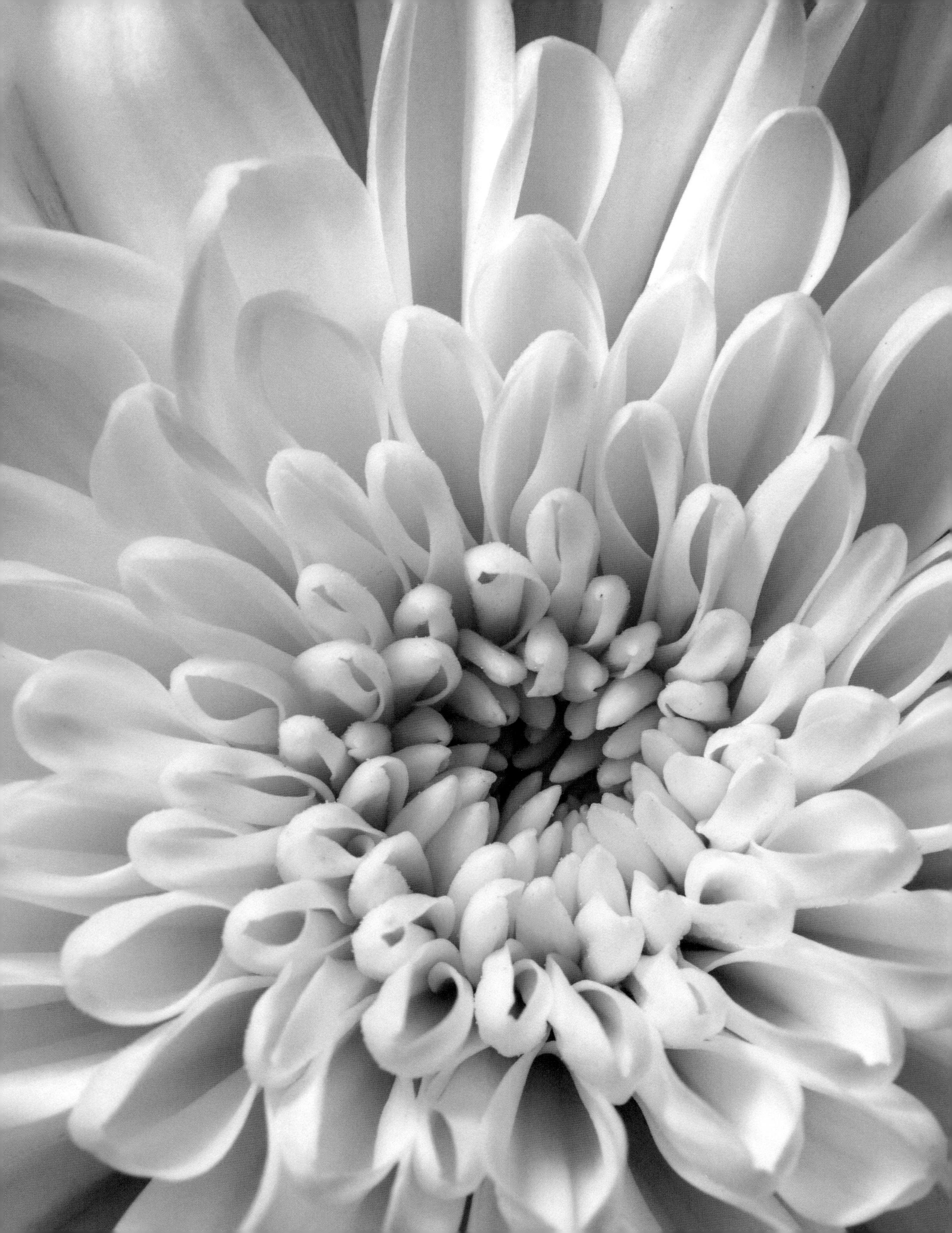

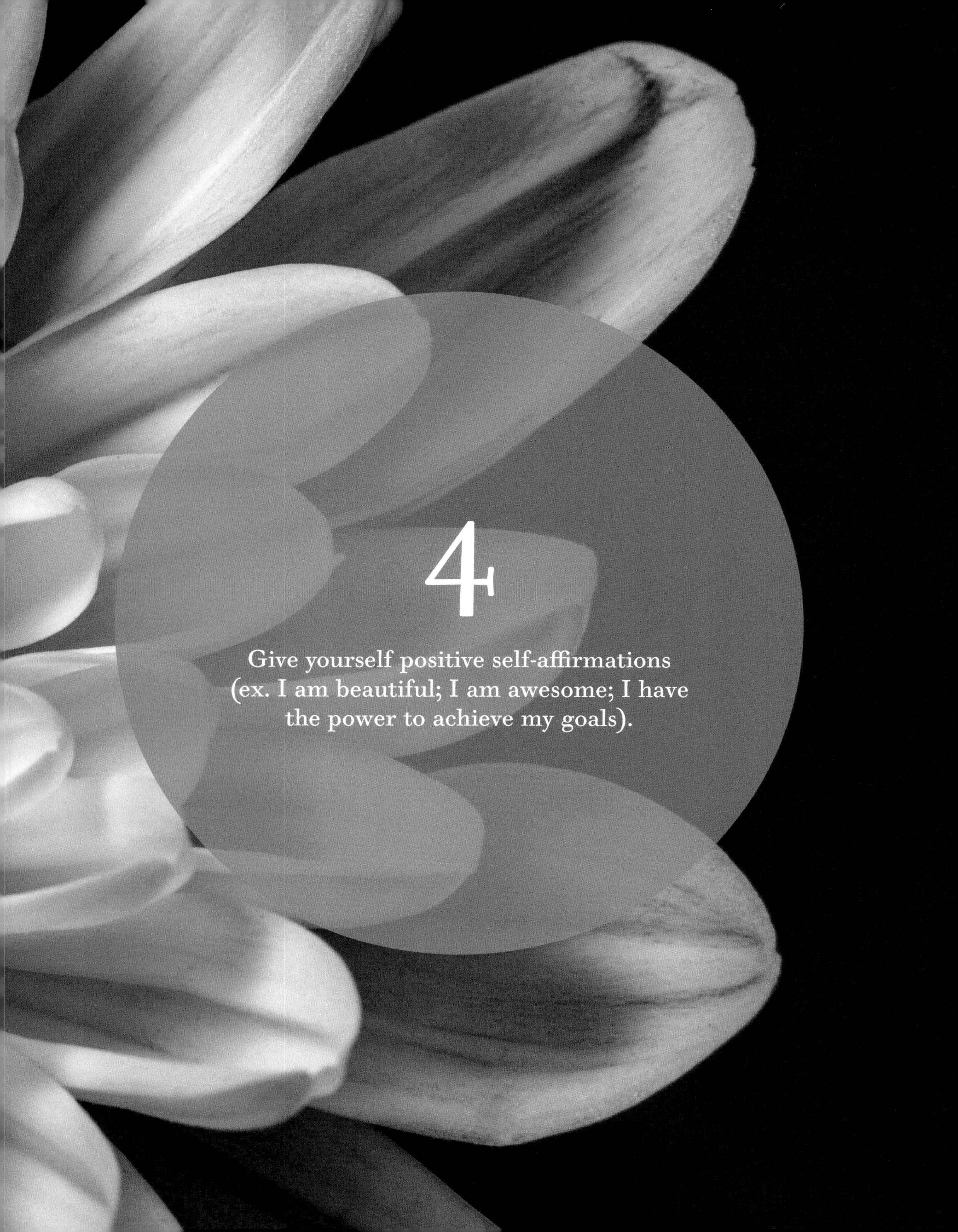

4

Give yourself positive self-affirmations (ex. I am beautiful; I am awesome; I have the power to achieve my goals).

Date
....

Thought/s:
....
....
....
....

Feeling/s:
....
....
....
....

Behavior/s:
....
....
....
....

Goal/s:
....
....
....
....

Date

Notes

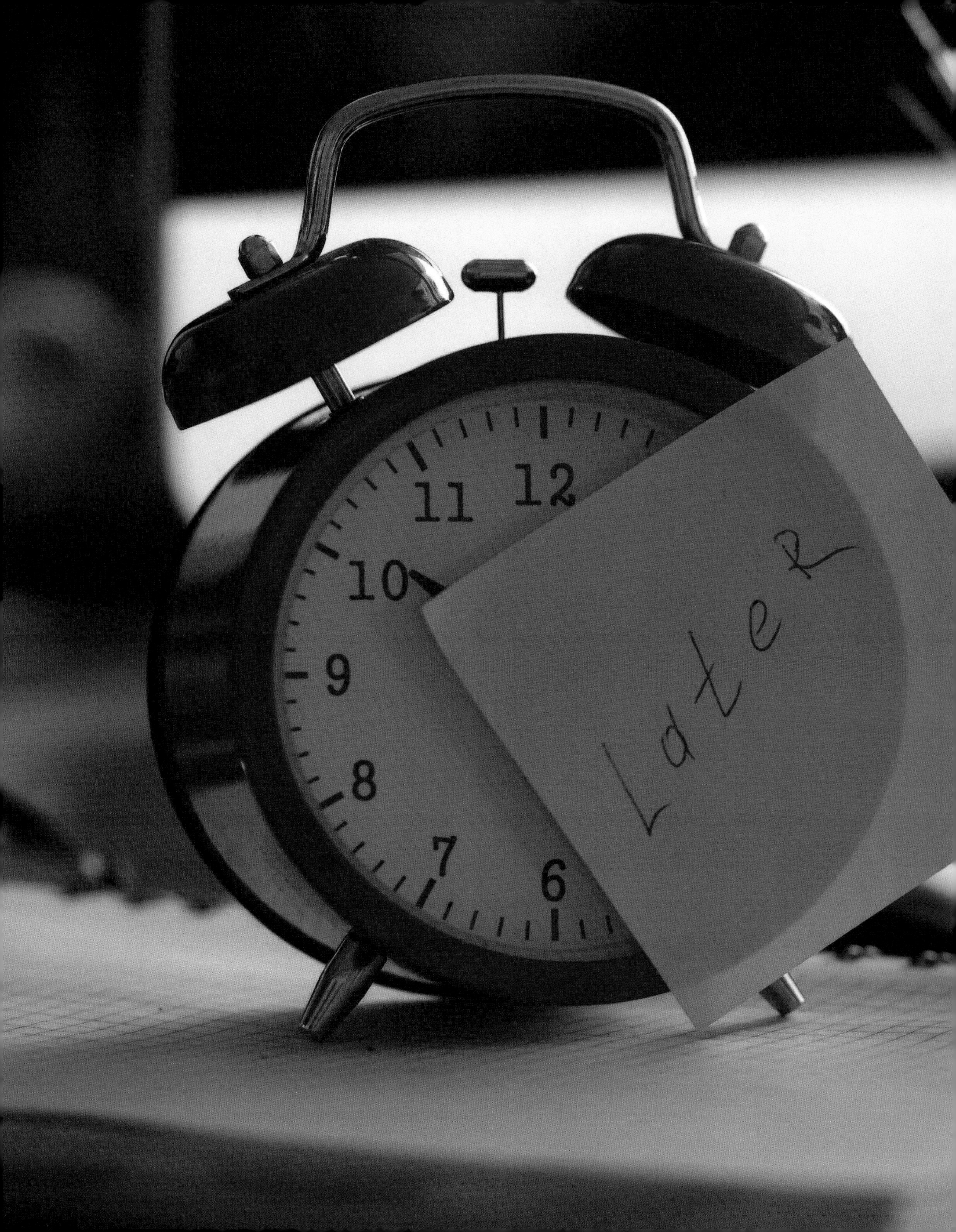
Later

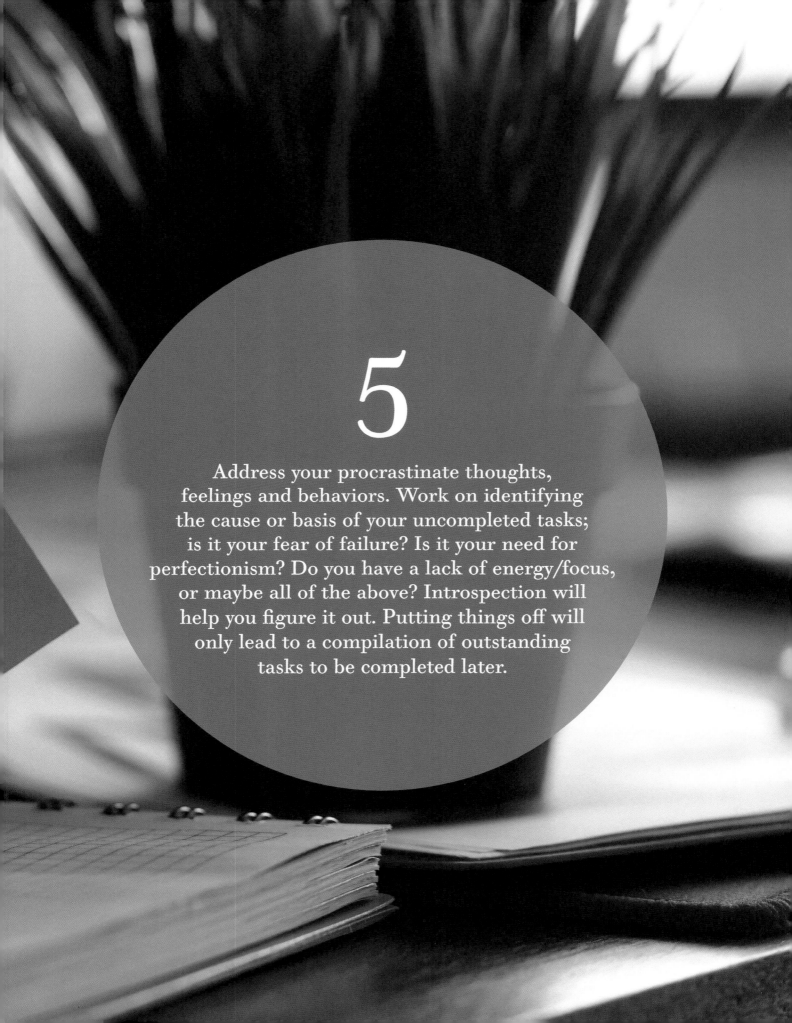

5

Address your procrastinate thoughts, feelings and behaviors. Work on identifying the cause or basis of your uncompleted tasks; is it your fear of failure? Is it your need for perfectionism? Do you have a lack of energy/focus, or maybe all of the above? Introspection will help you figure it out. Putting things off will only lead to a compilation of outstanding tasks to be completed later.

Date
....

Thought/s:
....
....
....
....

Feeling/s:
....
....
....
....

Behavior/s:
....
....
....
....

Goal/s:
....
....
....
....

Date

Notes

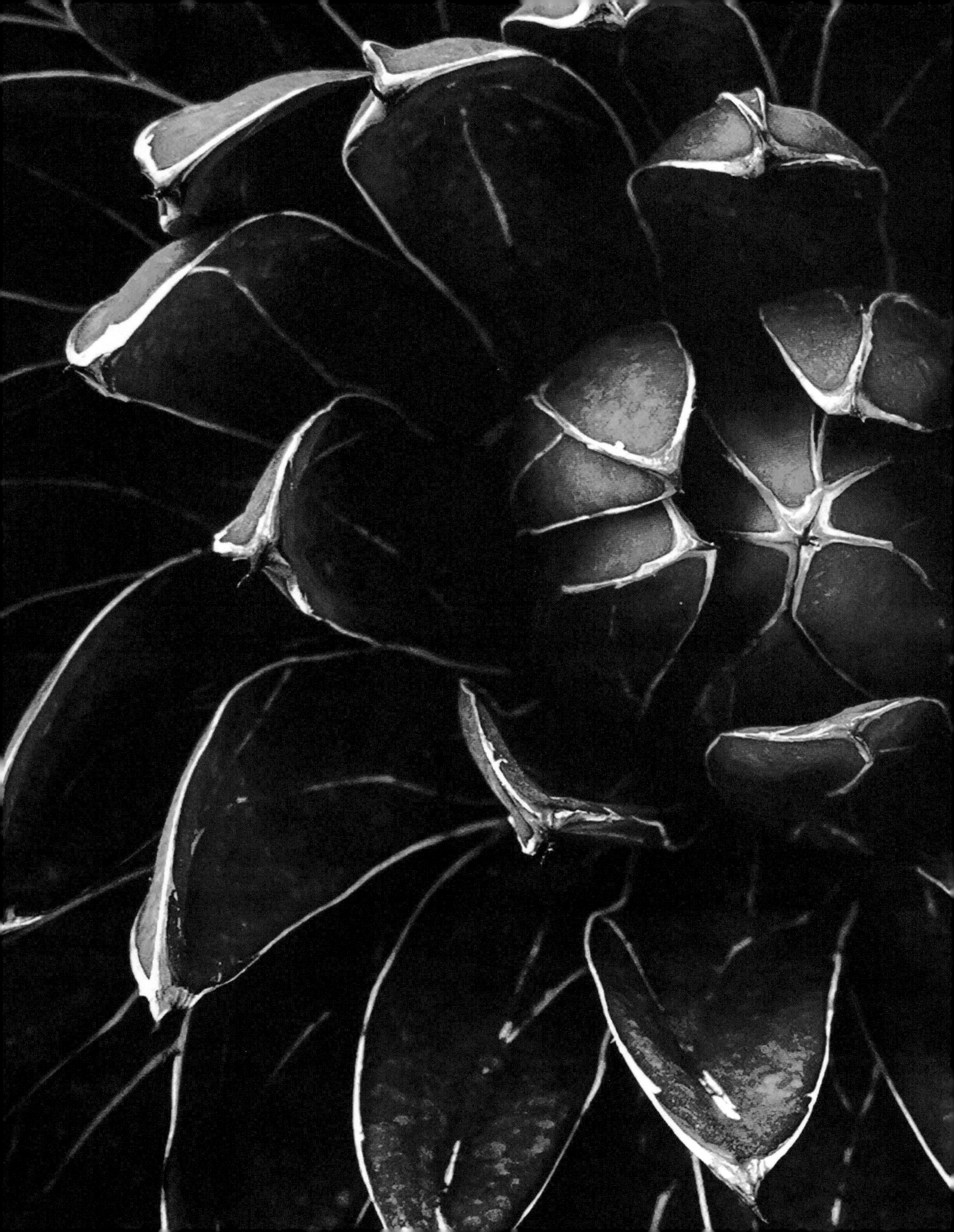

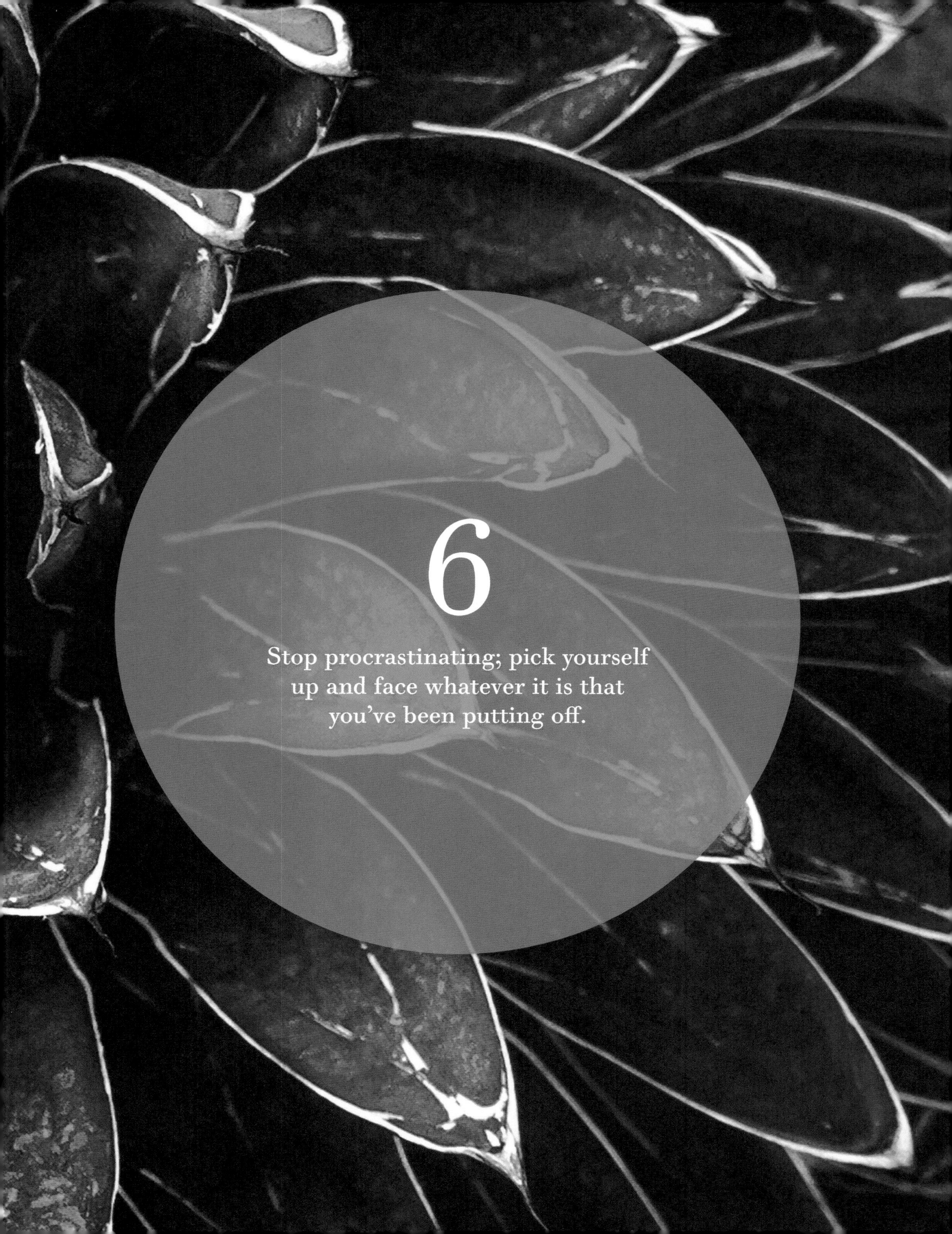

6

Stop procrastinating; pick yourself up and face whatever it is that you've been putting off.

Date
....

Thought/s:
....
....
....
....

Feeling/s:
....
....
....
....
....

Behavior/s:
....
....
....
....

Goal/s:
....
....
....
....

Date

Notes

35

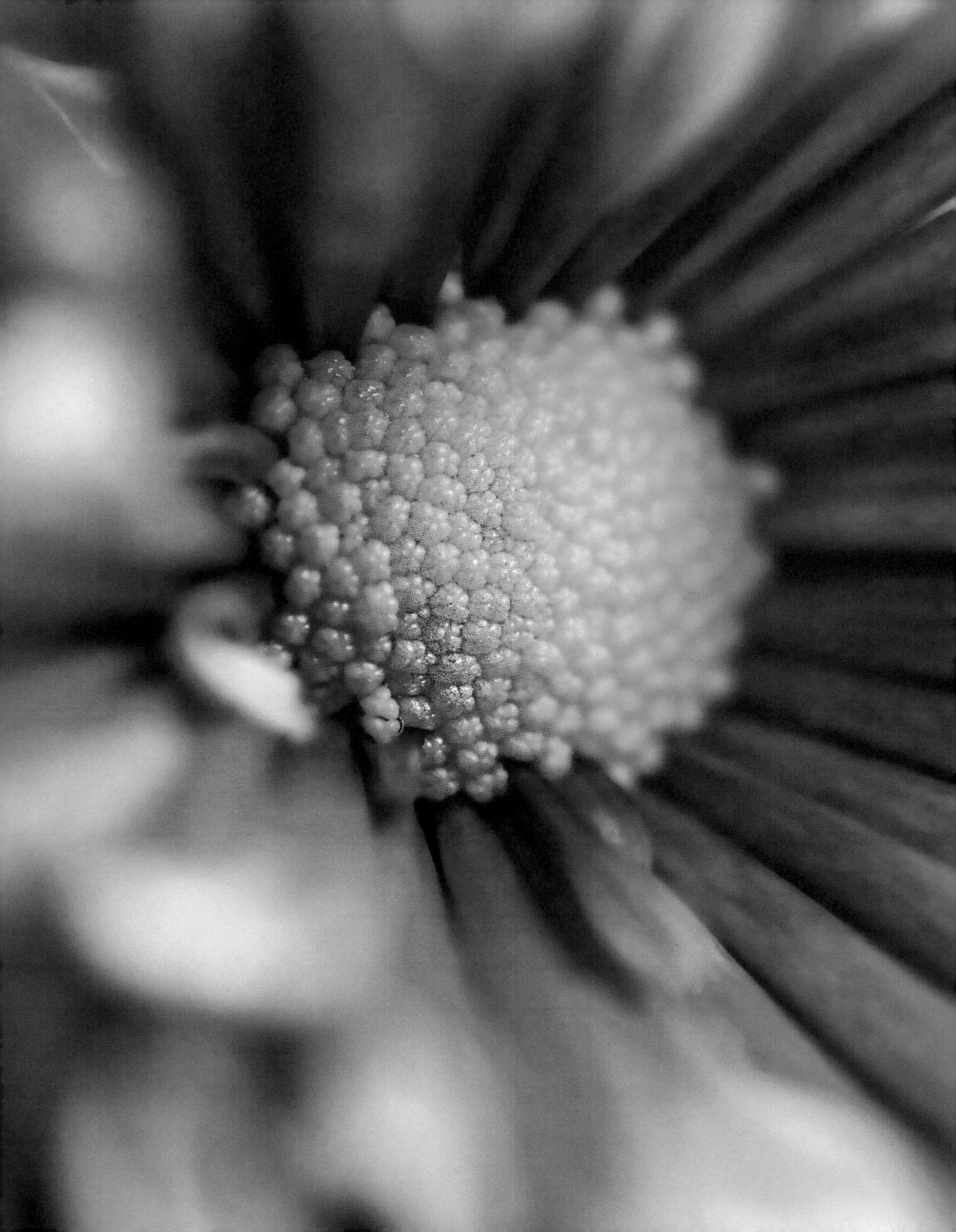

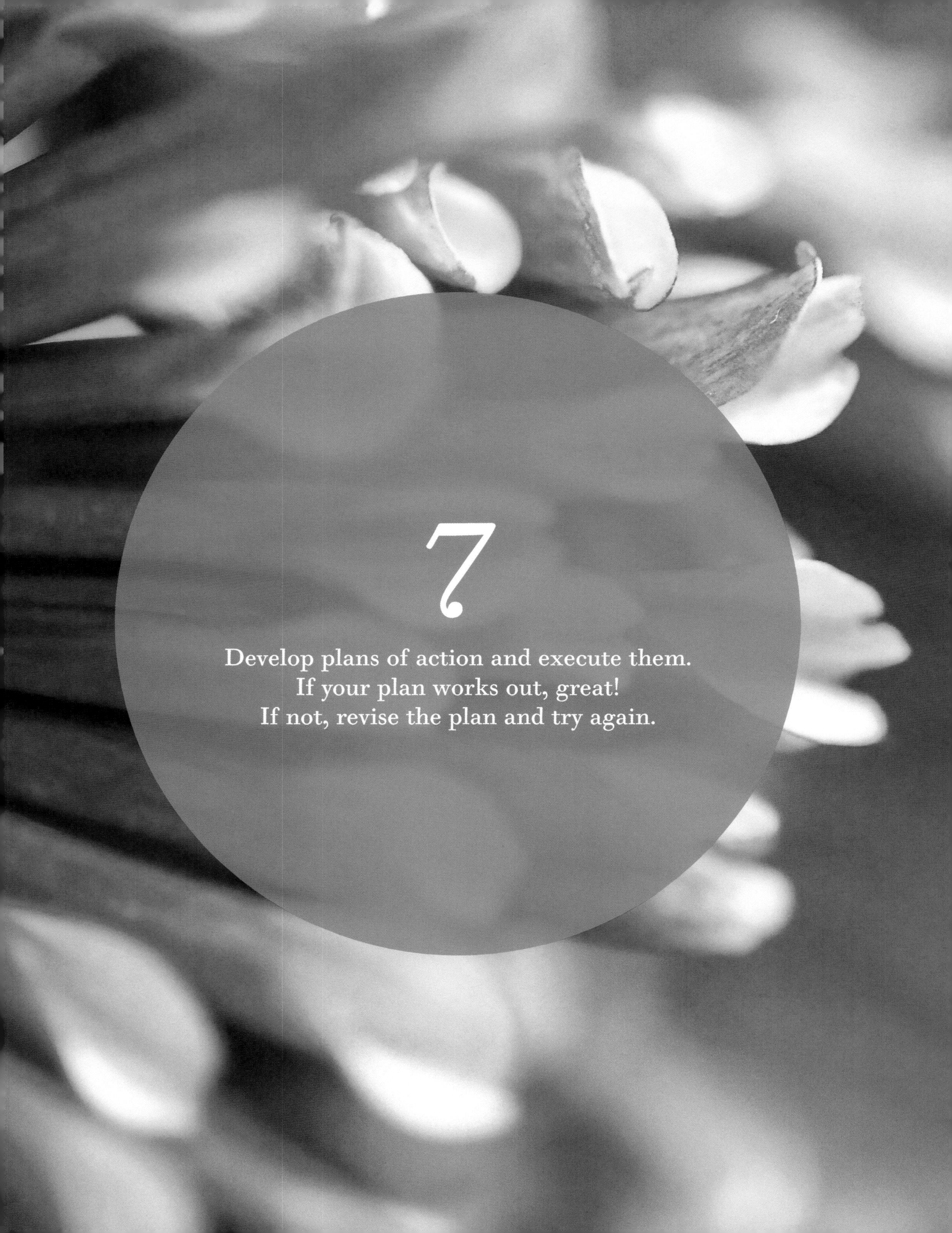

7

Develop plans of action and execute them.
If your plan works out, great!
If not, revise the plan and try again.

Date
....

Thought/s:
....
....
....
....

Feeling/s:
....
....
....
....

Behavior/s:
....
....
....
....

Goal/s:
....
....
....
....

Date

Notes

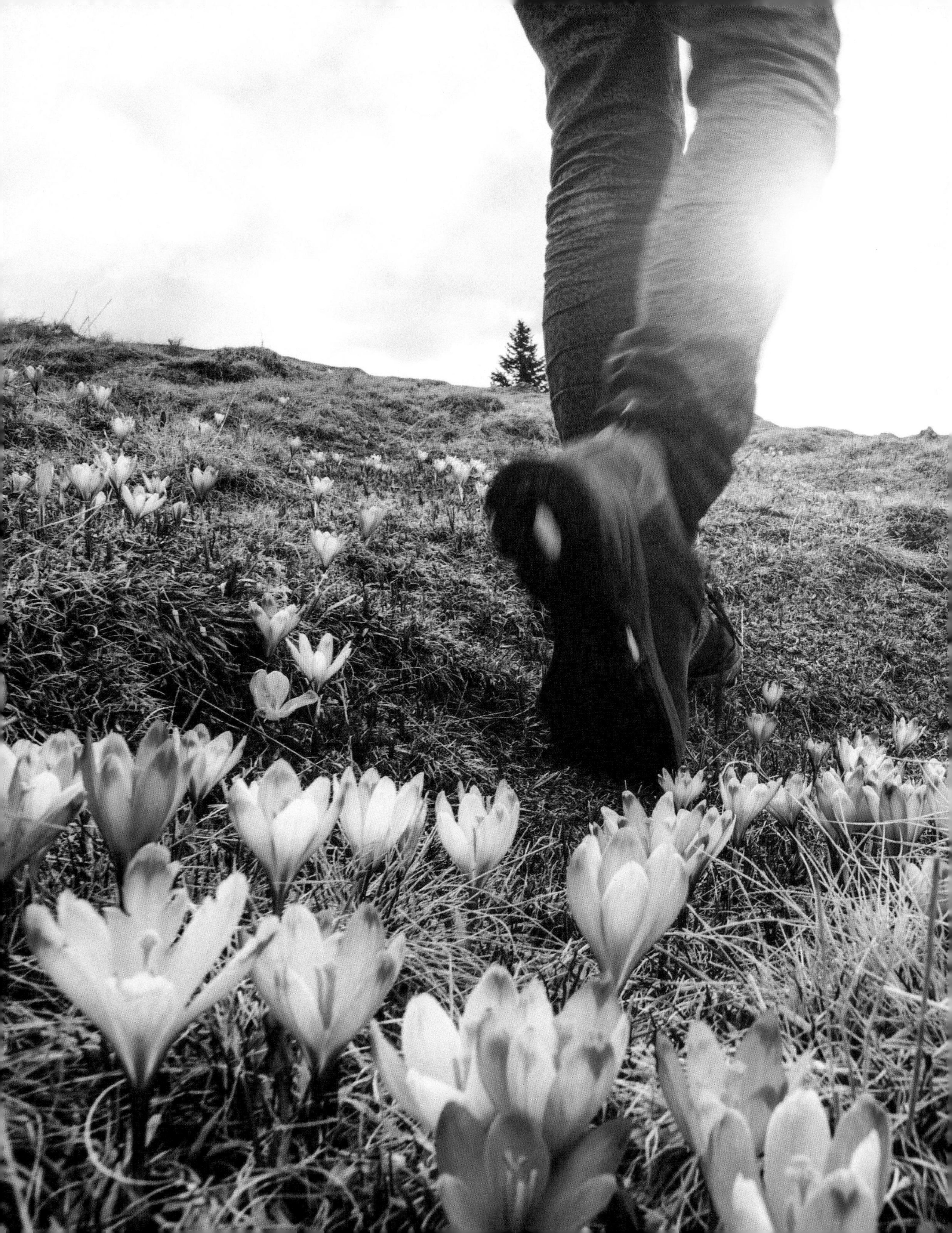

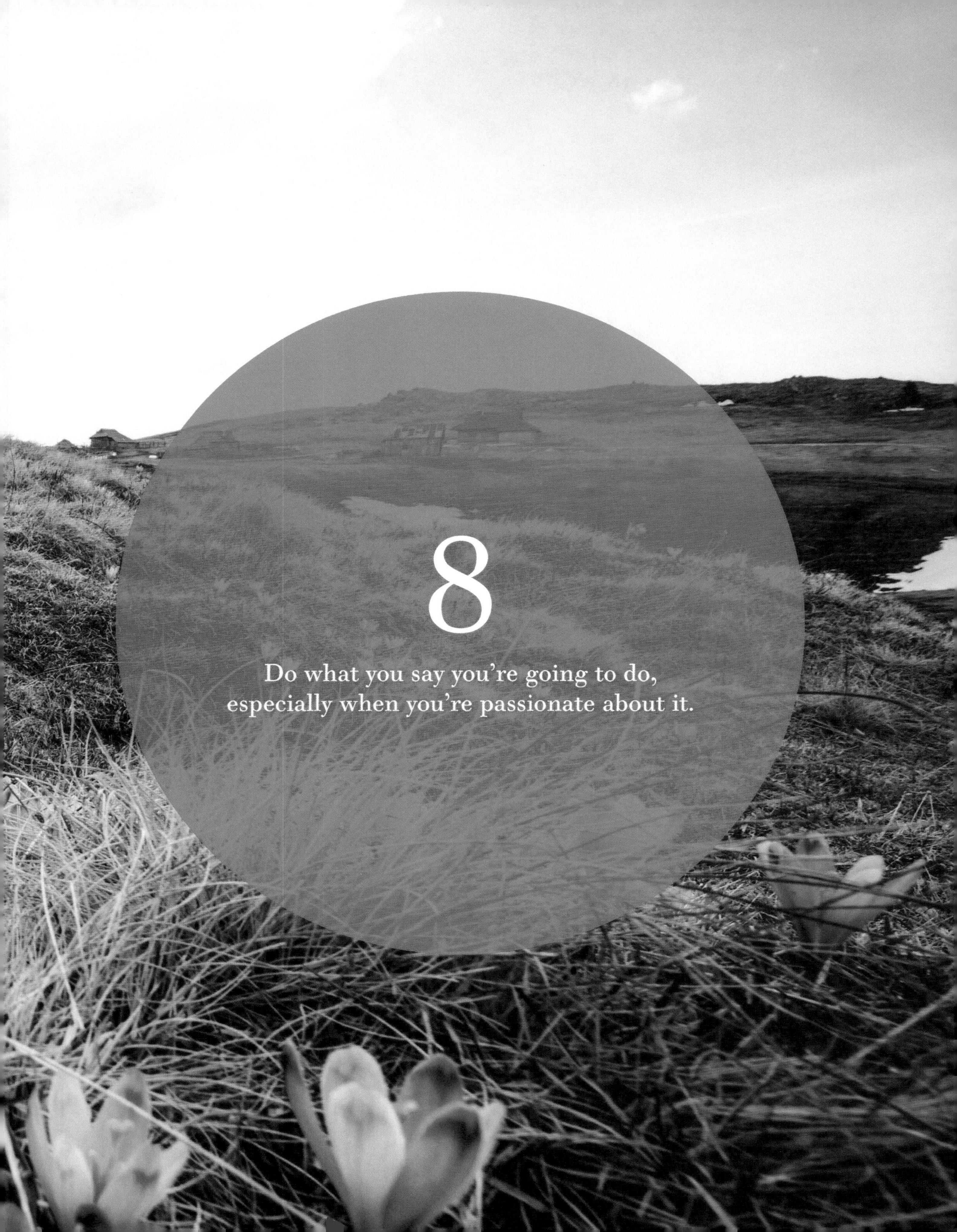

8

Do what you say you're going to do,
especially when you're passionate about it.

Date
....

Thought/s:
....
....
....
....

Feeling/s:
....
....
....
....

Behavior/s:
....
....
....
....

Goal/s:
....
....
....
....

Date

Notes

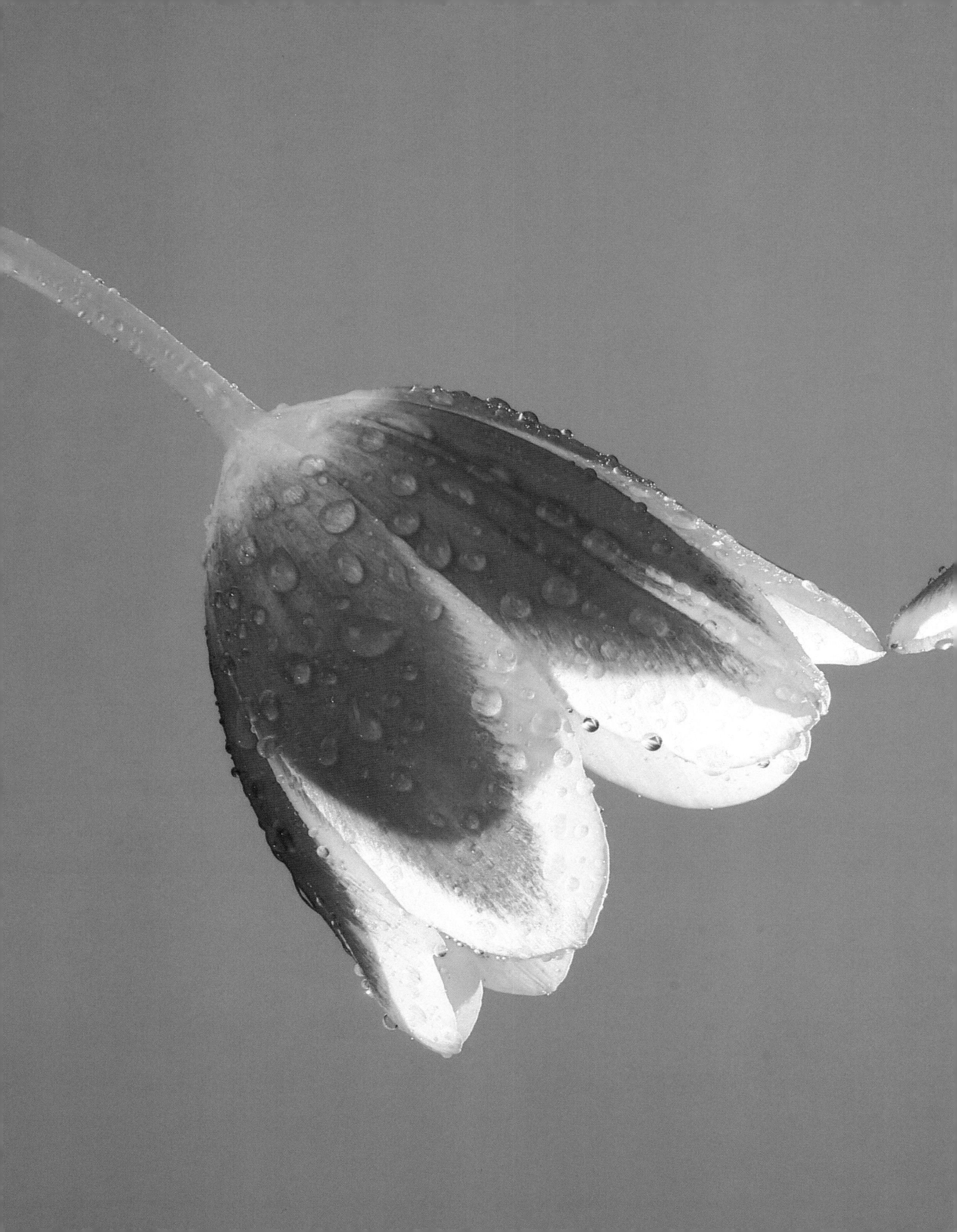

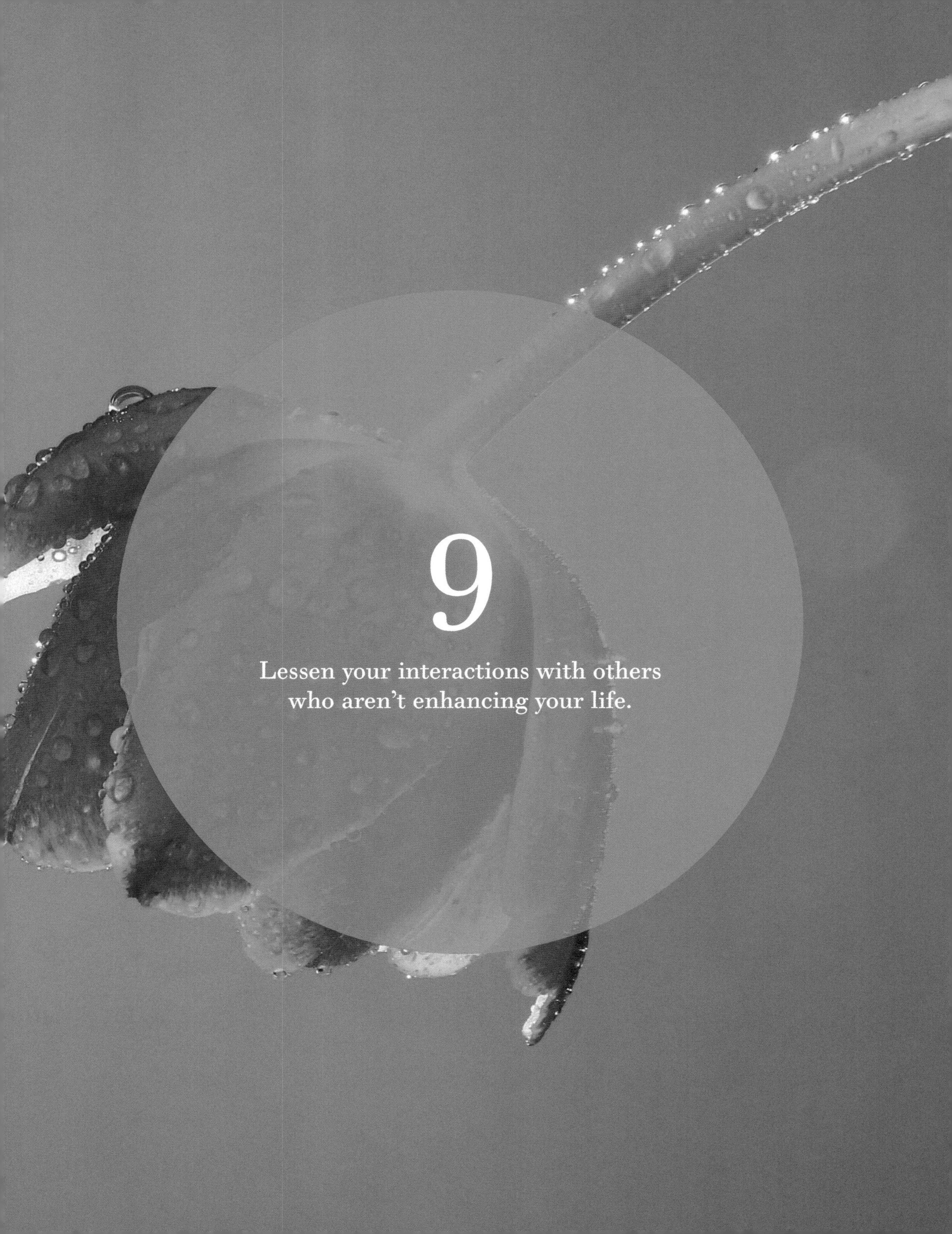

9

Lessen your interactions with others
who aren't enhancing your life.

Date

Thought/s:

Feeling/s:

Behavior/s:

Goal/s:

Date

Notes

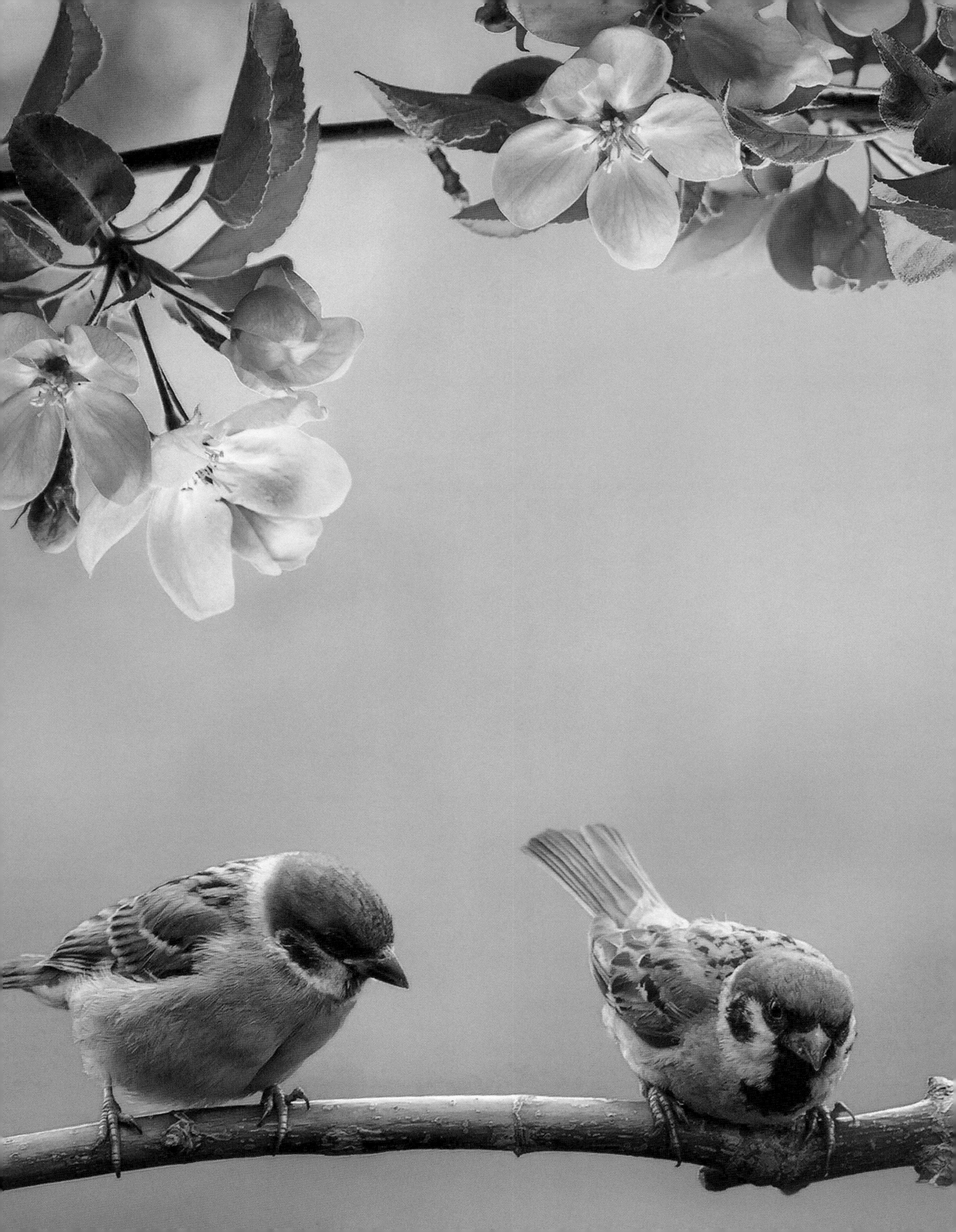

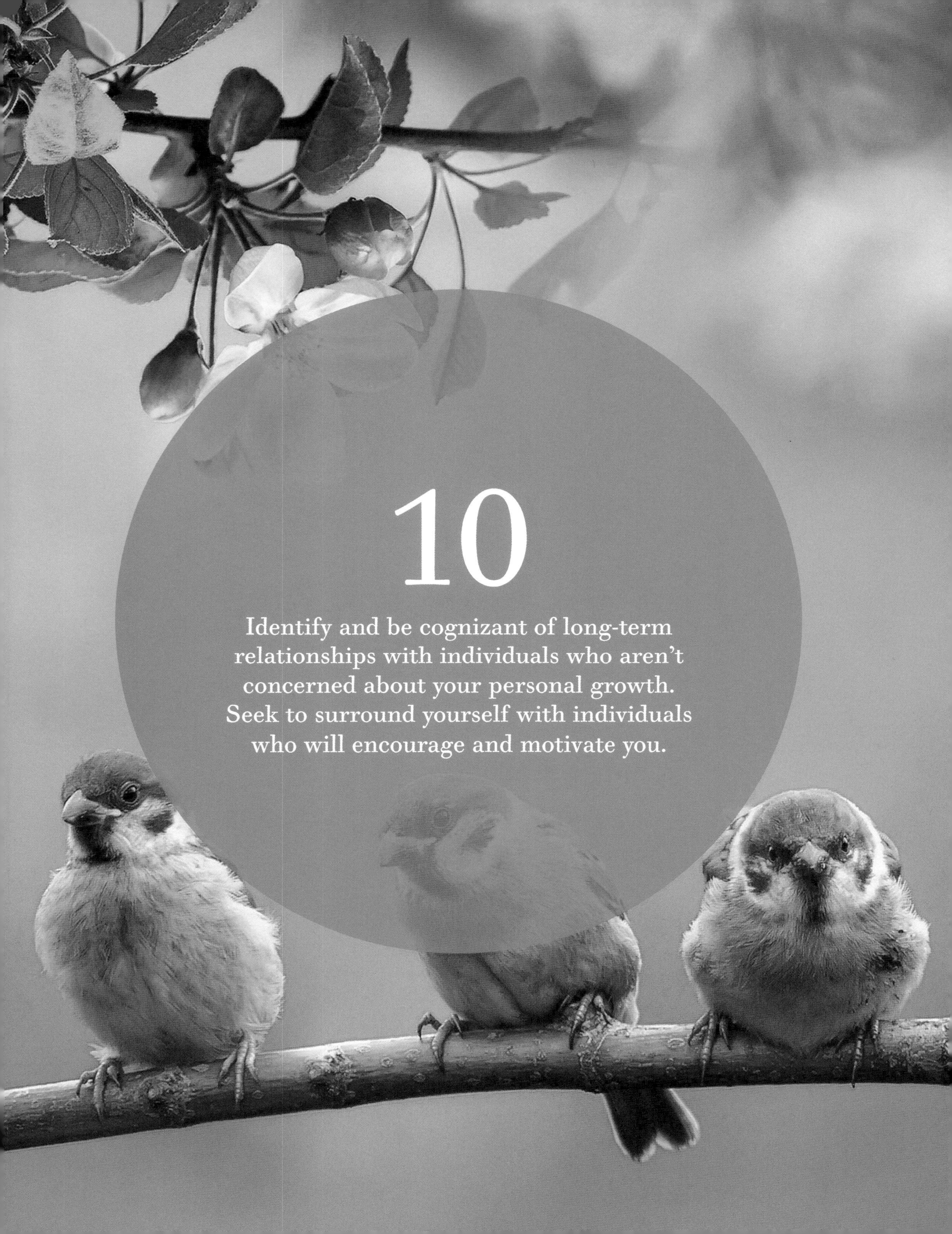

10

Identify and be cognizant of long-term relationships with individuals who aren't concerned about your personal growth. Seek to surround yourself with individuals who will encourage and motivate you.

Date

Thought/s:

Feeling/s:

Behavior/s:

Goal/s:

Date

Notes

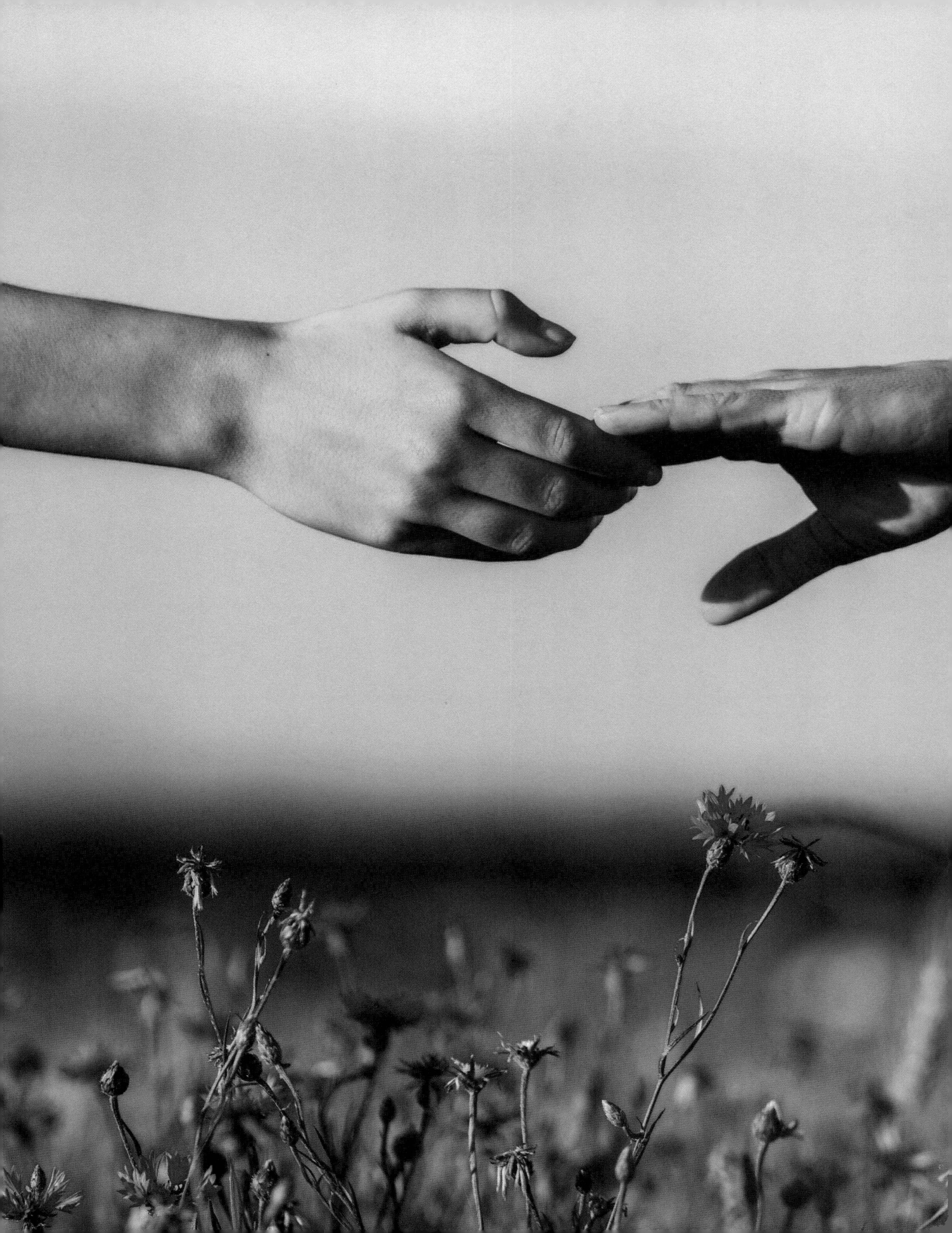

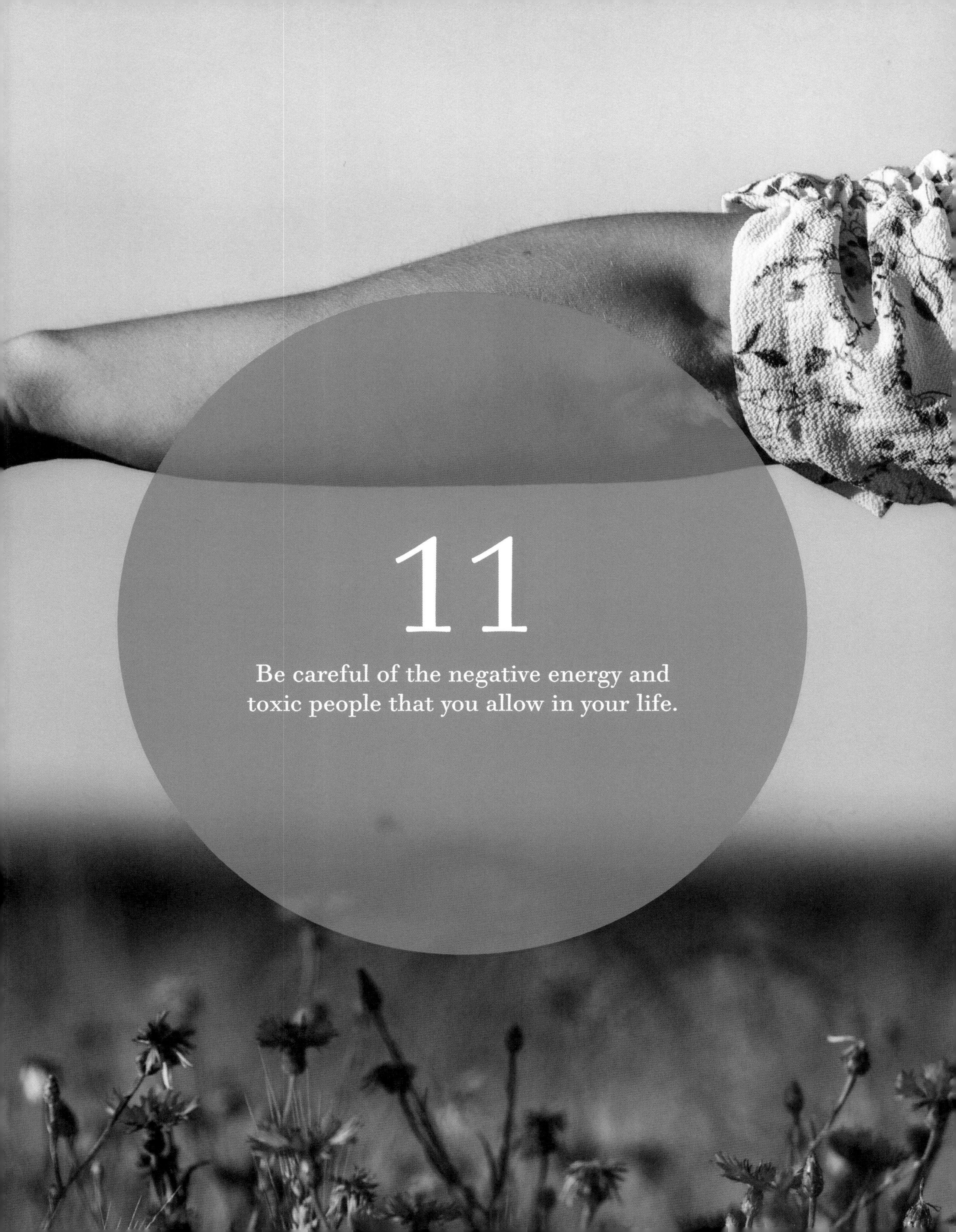

11

Be careful of the negative energy and toxic people that you allow in your life.

Date
....

Thought/s:
....
....
....
....

Feeling/s:
....
....
....
....

Behavior/s:
....
....
....
....

Goal/s:
....
....
....
....

Date

Notes

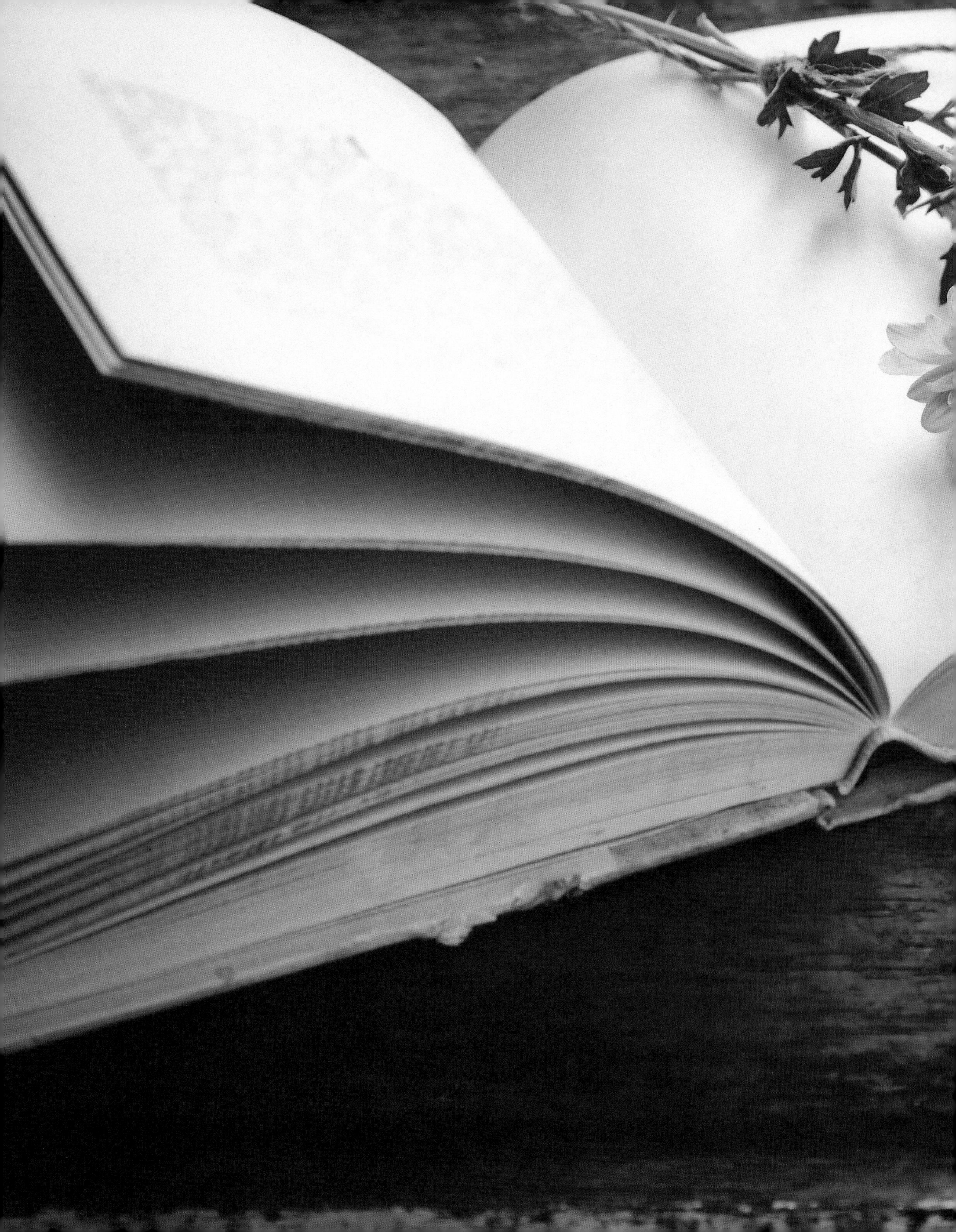

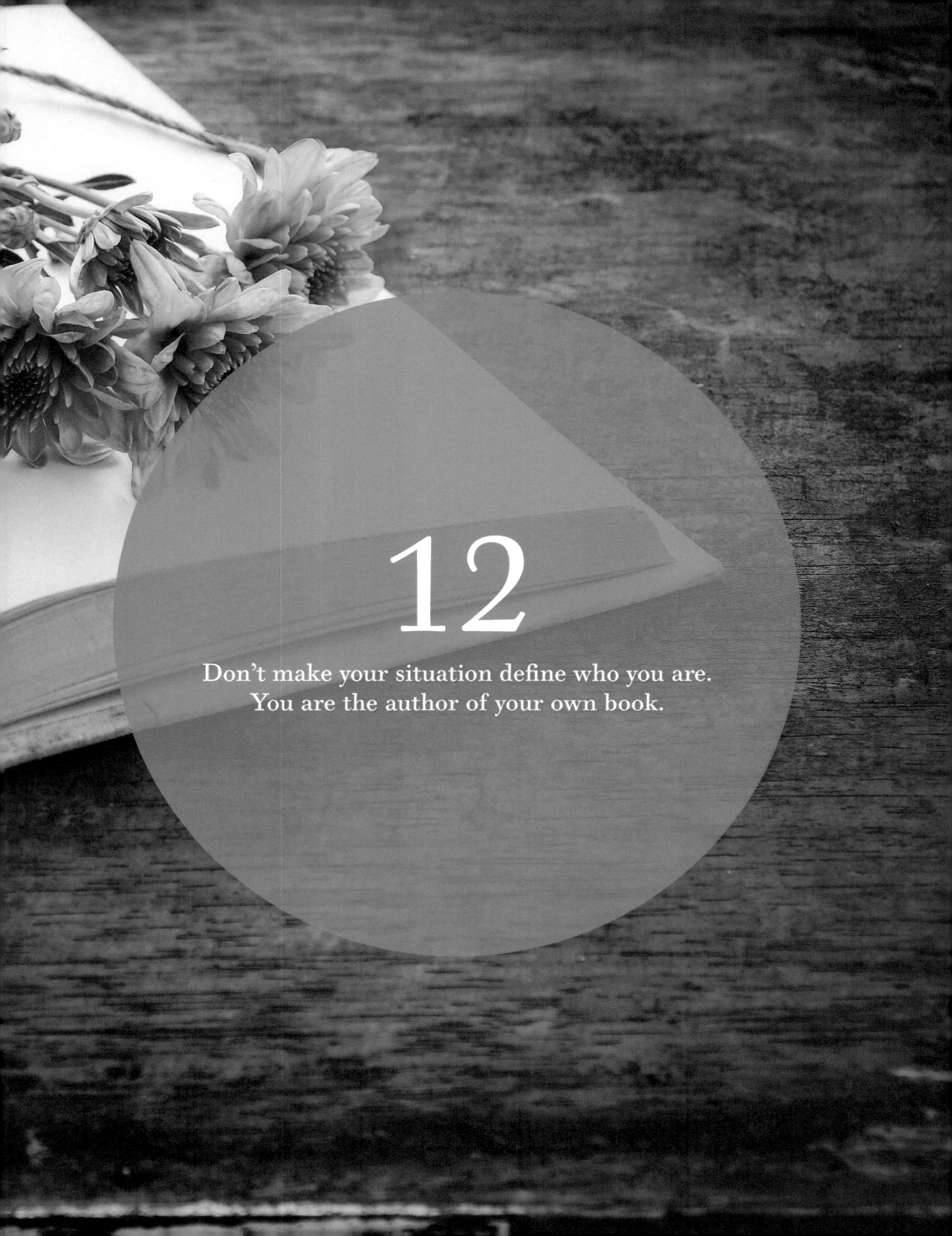

12

Don't make your situation define who you are.
You are the author of your own book.

Date
....

Thought/s:
....
....
....

Feeling/s:
....
....
....
....

Behavior/s:
....
....
....
....

Goal/s:
....
....
....
....

Date
....

Notes
....

....

....

....

....

....

....

....

....

....

....

....

....

....

....

....

....

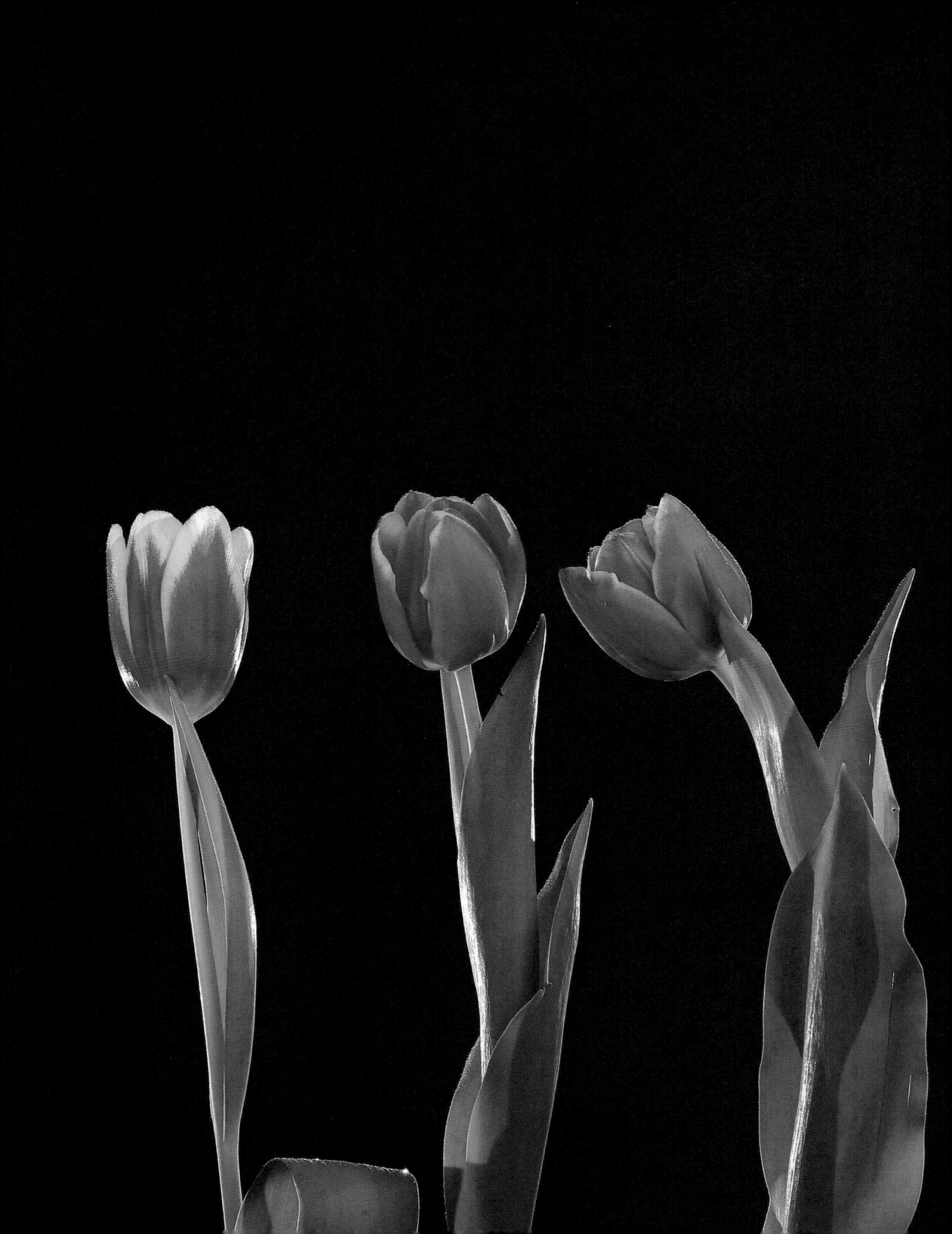

13

Keep your business to yourself. If you have plans to advance yourself, don't share it with everyone; negative energy is transferable.

Date
....

Thought/s:
....

....

....

....

Feeling/s:
....

....

....

....

Behavior/s:
....

....

....

....

Goal/s:
....

....

....

....

Date

Notes

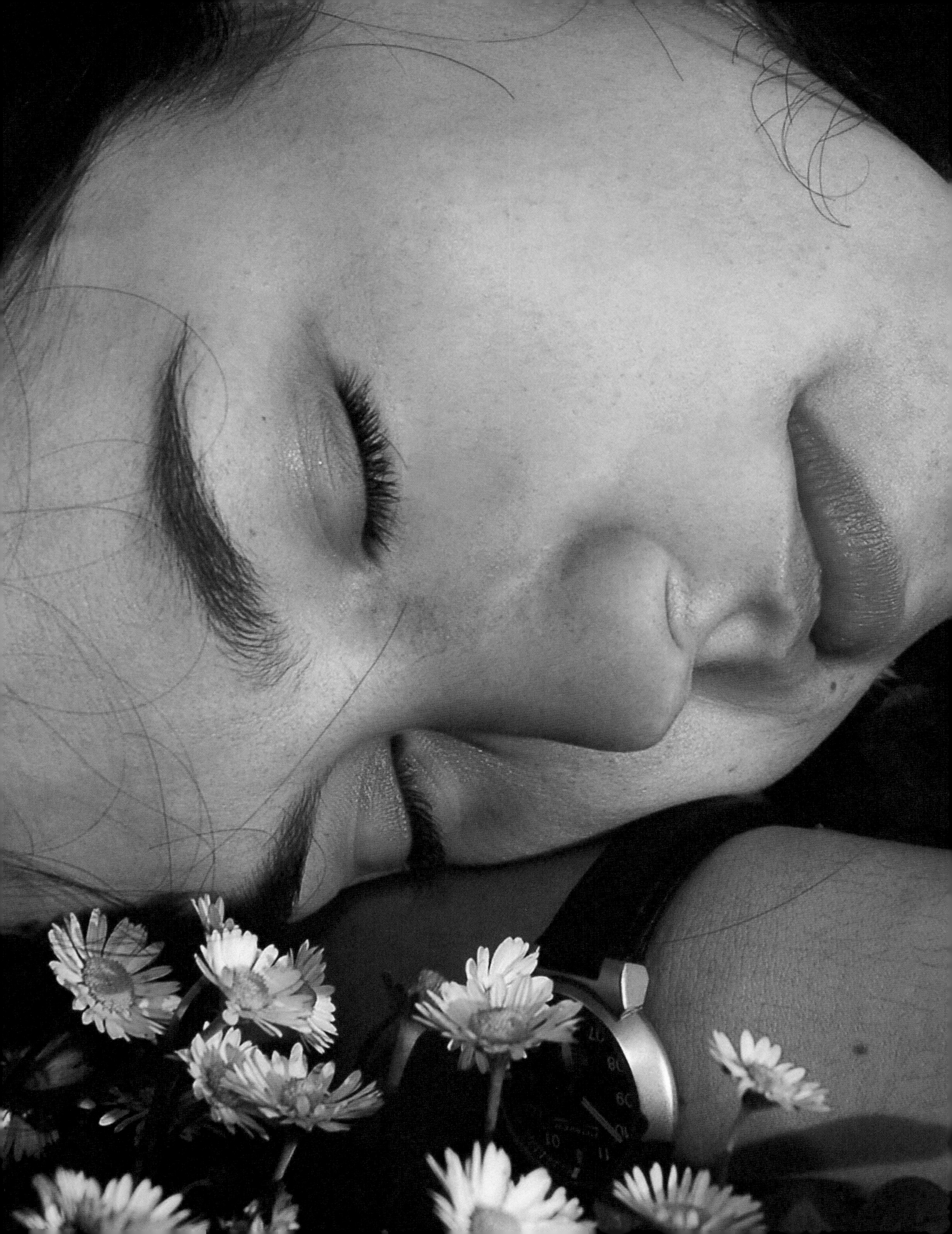

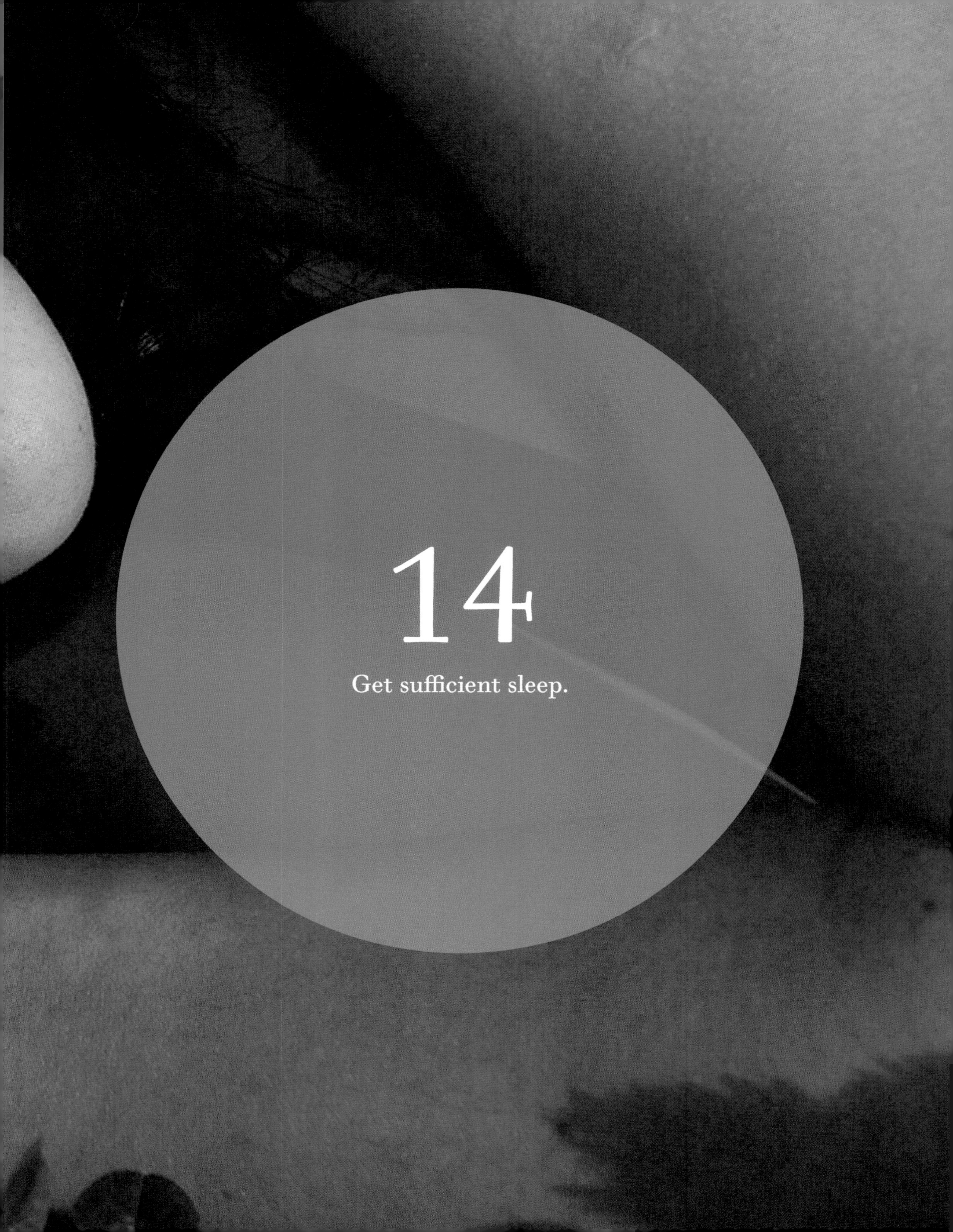

14

Get sufficient sleep.

Date
....

Thought/s:
....
....
....
....

Feeling/s:
....
....
....
....
....

Behavior/s:
....
....
....
....

Goal/s:
....
....
....
....

Date

Notes

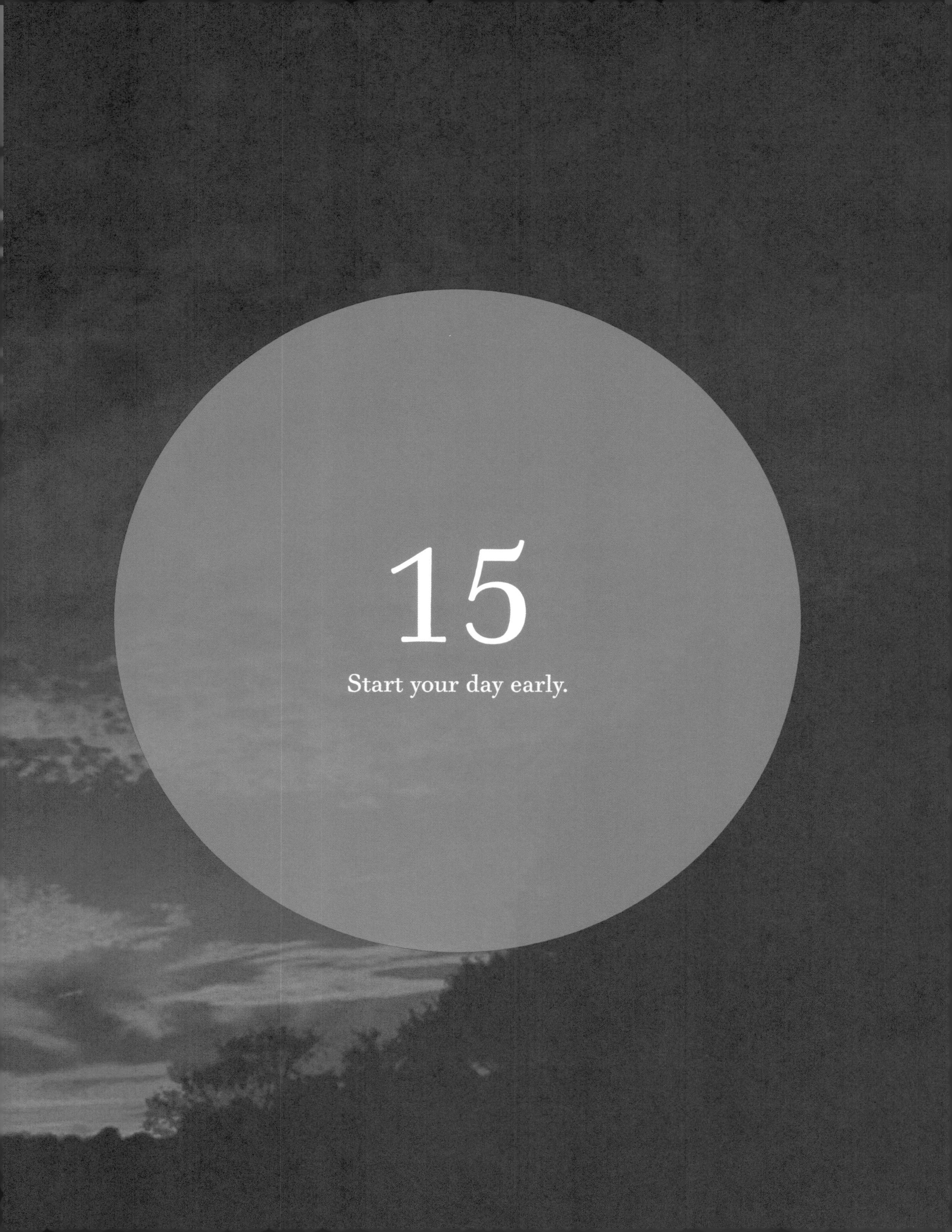

15

Start your day early.

Date
....

Thought/s:
....
....
....
....

Feeling/s:
....
....
....
....
....

Behavior/s:
....
....
....
....

Goal/s:
....
....
....
....

Date

Notes

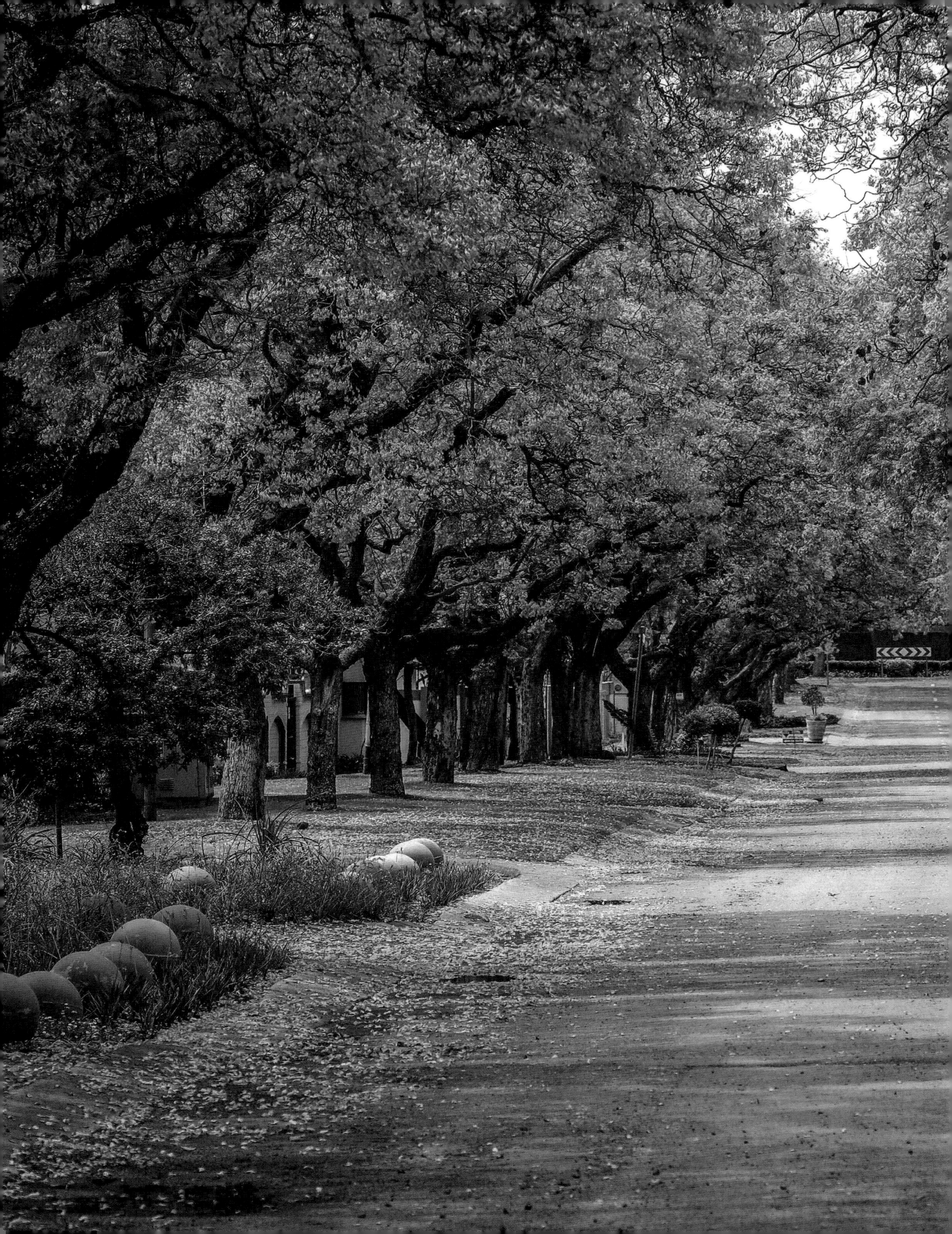

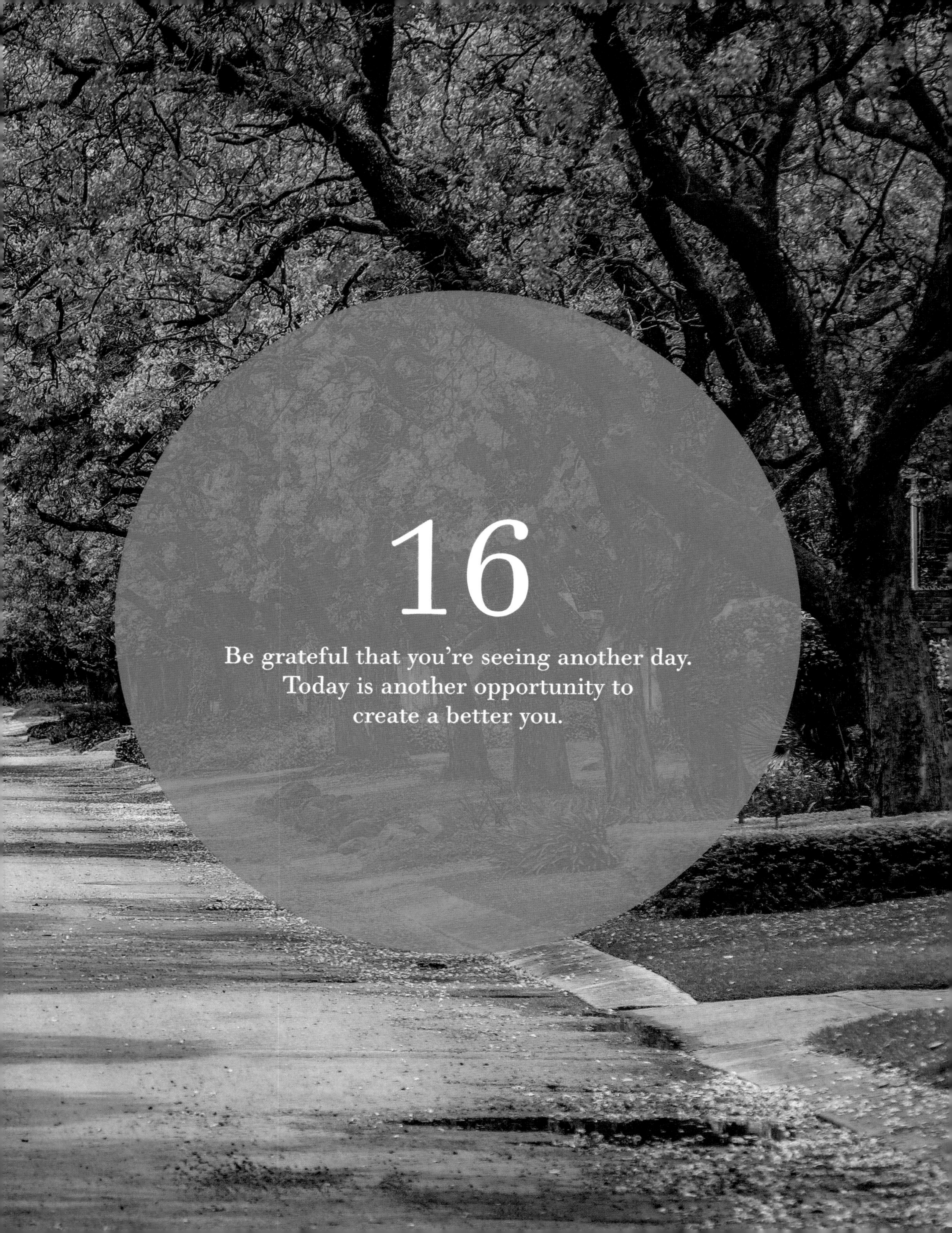

16

Be grateful that you're seeing another day.
Today is another opportunity to
create a better you.

Date
....

Thought/s:
....
....
....
....

Feeling/s:
....
....
....
....

Behavior/s:
....
....
....
....

Goal/s:
....
....
....
....

Date

Notes

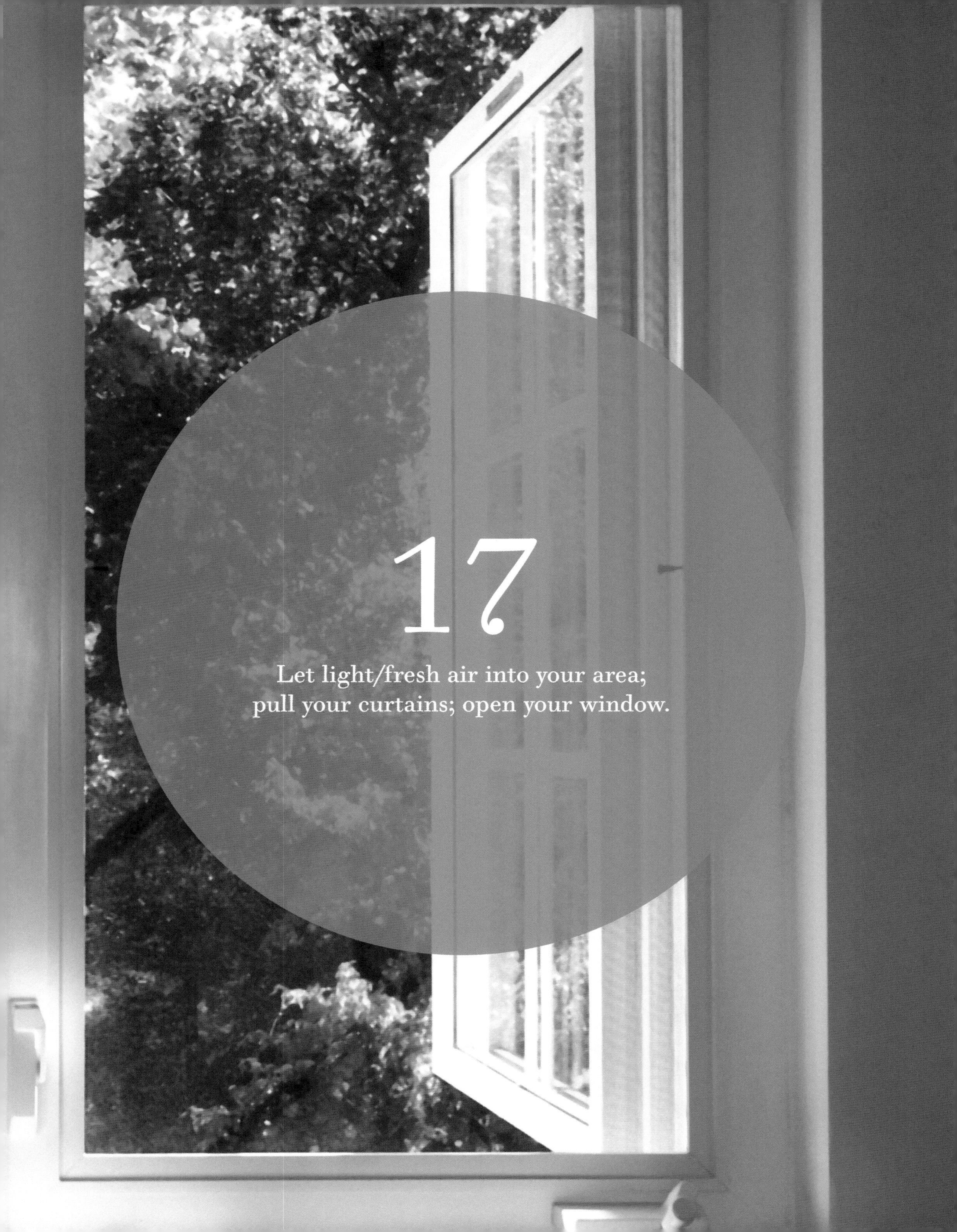

17

Let light/fresh air into your area;
pull your curtains; open your window.

Date

....

Thought/s:

....

....

....

....

Feeling/s:

....

....

....

....

Behavior/s:

....

....

....

....

Goal/s:

....

....

....

....

Date
....

Notes
....
....
....
....
....
....
....
....
....
....
....
....
....
....
....
....

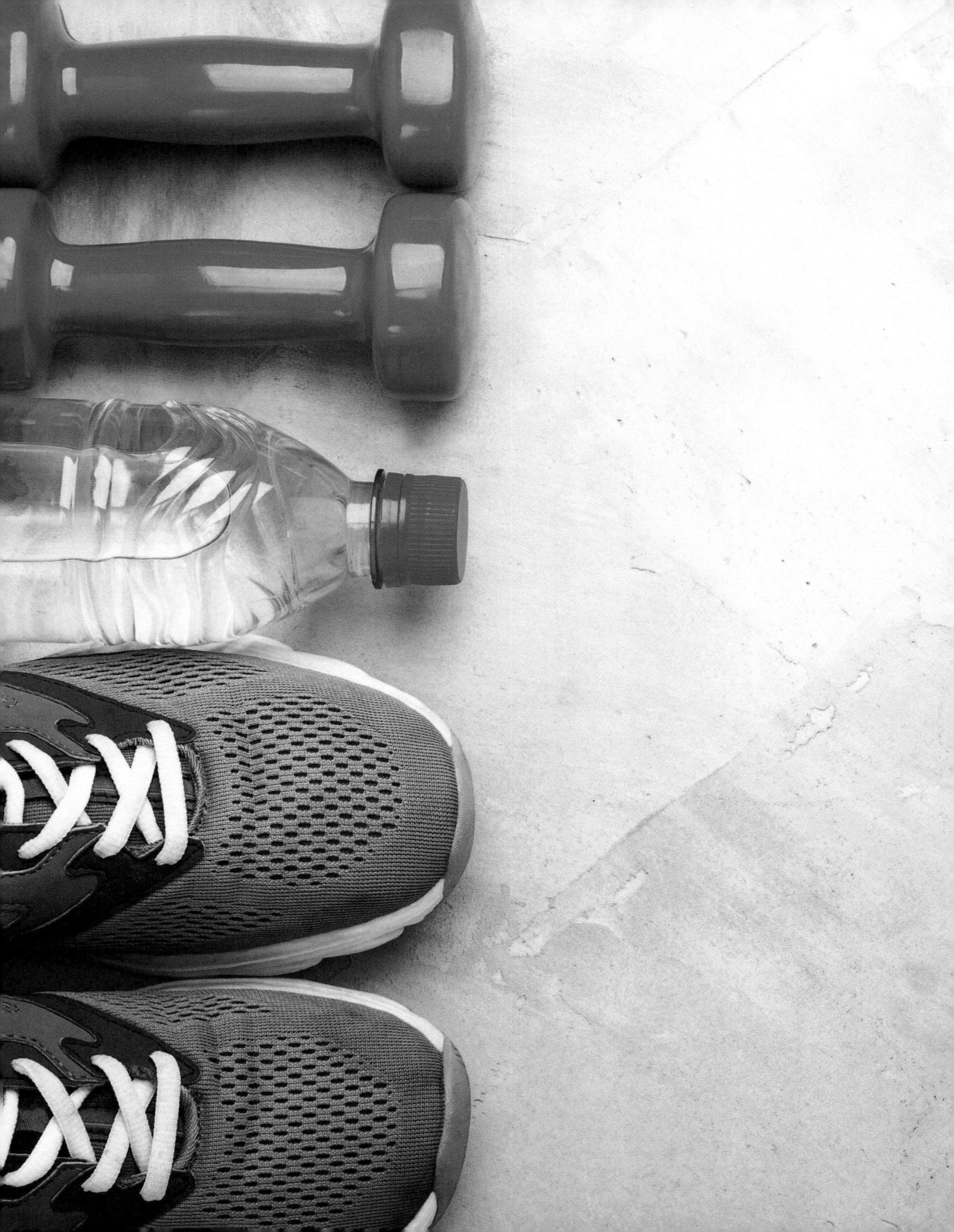

18

Exercise for at least thirty minutes (at least three times per week; consult with your doctor first).

Date

....

Thought/s:

....

....

....

....

Feeling/s:

....

....

....

....

Behavior/s:

....

....

....

....

Goal/s:

....

....

....

....

Date

Notes

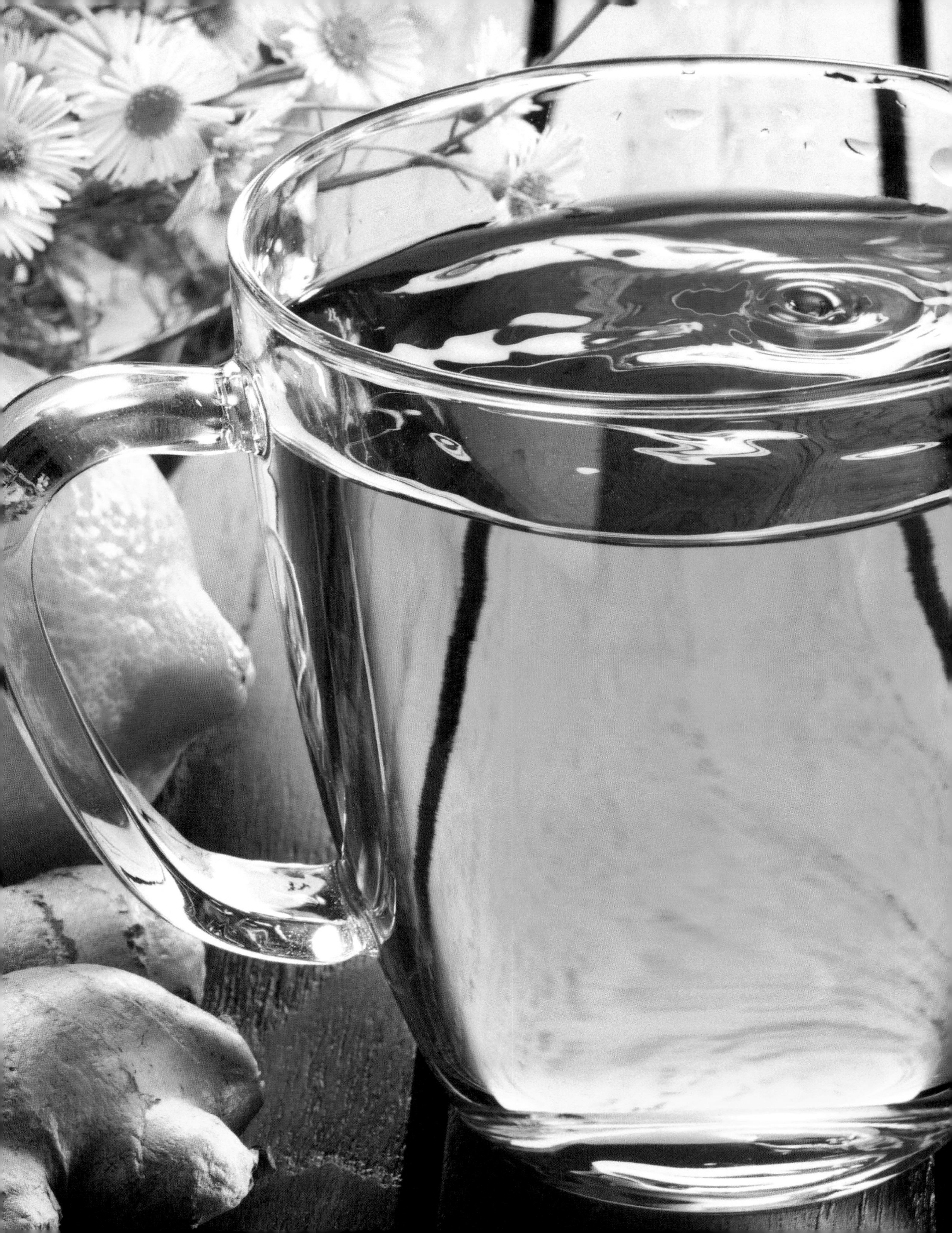

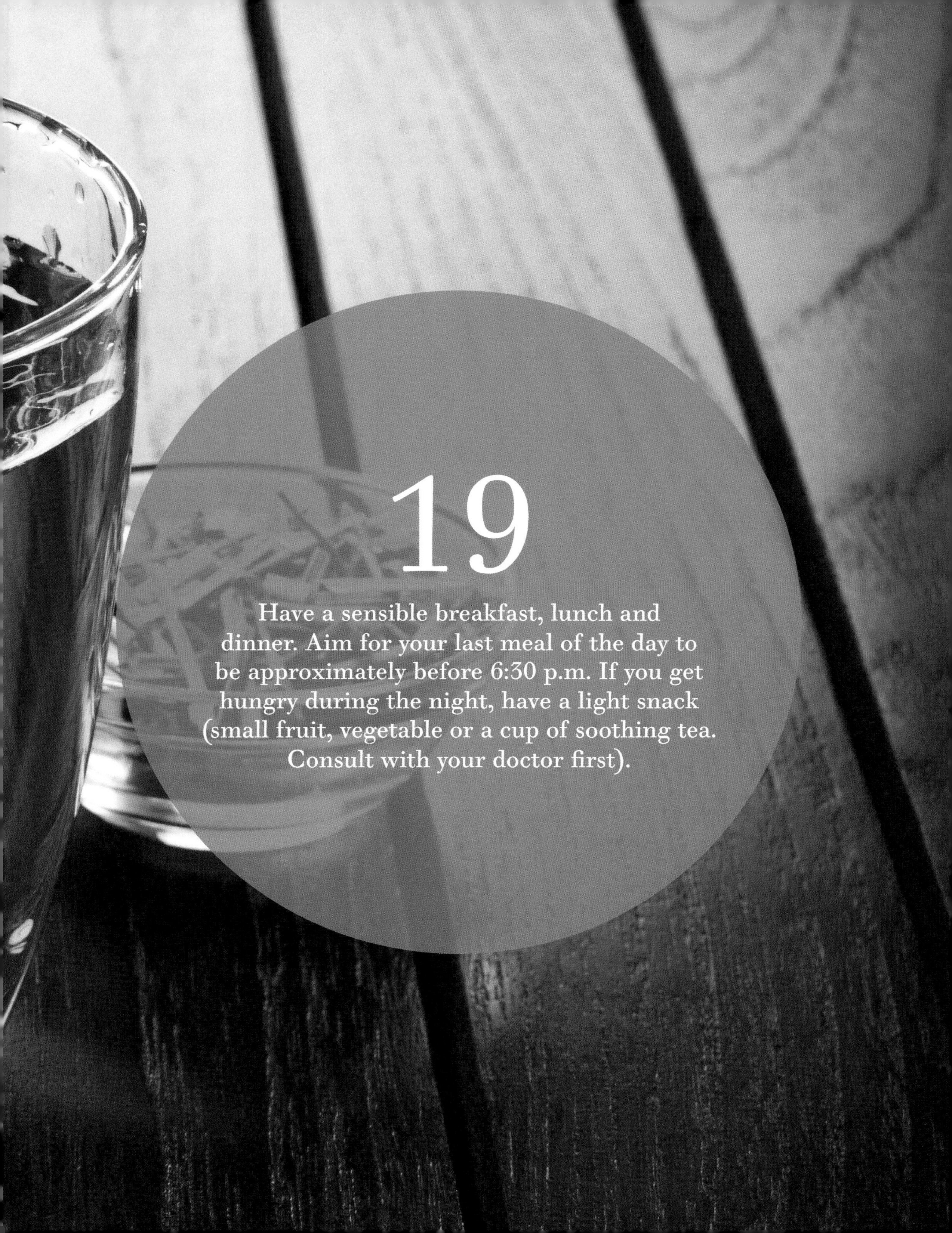

19

Have a sensible breakfast, lunch and dinner. Aim for your last meal of the day to be approximately before 6:30 p.m. If you get hungry during the night, have a light snack (small fruit, vegetable or a cup of soothing tea. Consult with your doctor first).

Date
....

Thought/s:
....
....
....
....

Feeling/s:
....
....
....
....
....

Behavior/s:
....
....
....
....

Goal/s:
....
....
....
....

Date

Notes

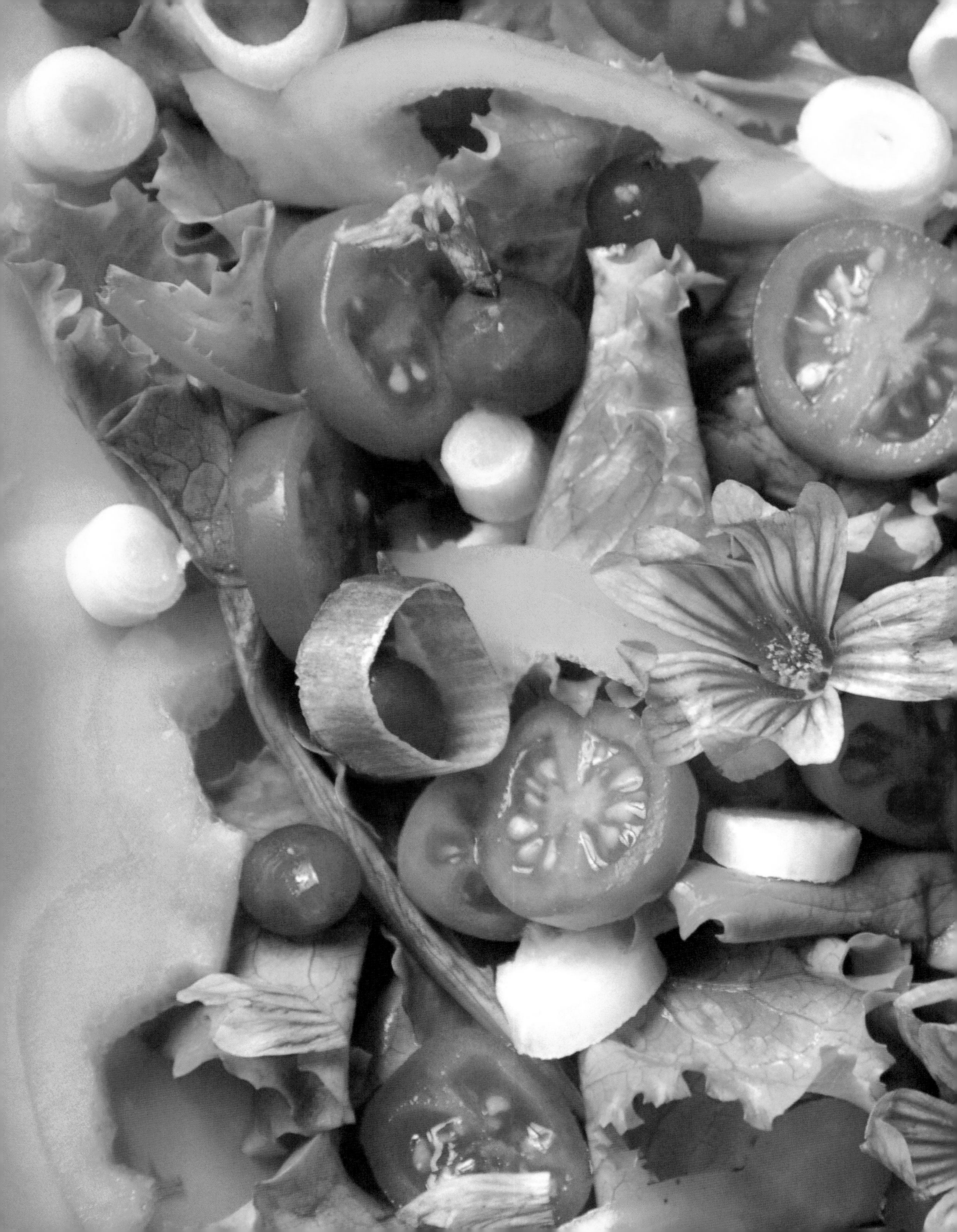

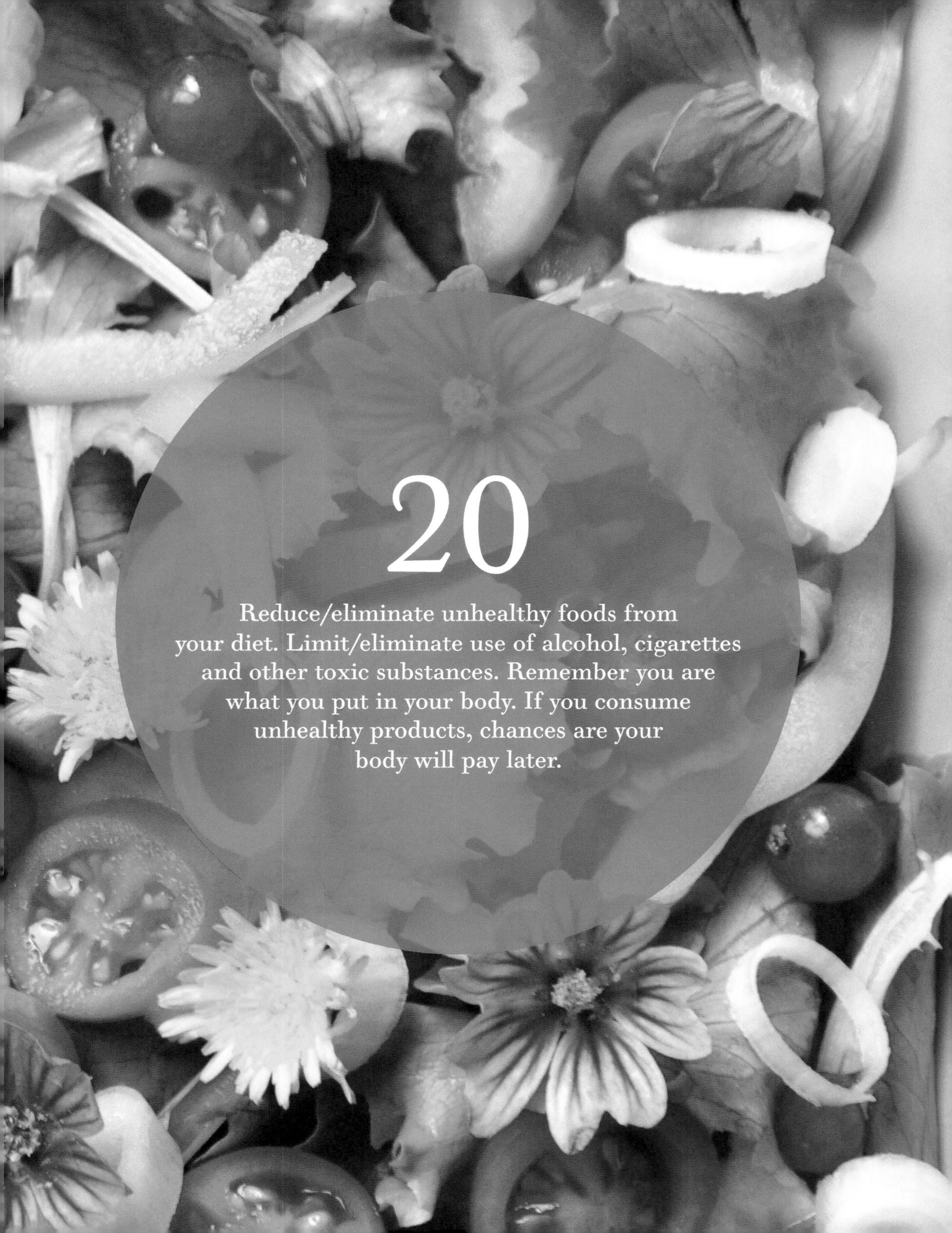

20

Reduce/eliminate unhealthy foods from your diet. Limit/eliminate use of alcohol, cigarettes and other toxic substances. Remember you are what you put in your body. If you consume unhealthy products, chances are your body will pay later.

Date
....

Thought/s:
....
....
....

Feeling/s:
....
....
....
....

Behavior/s:
....
....
....

Goal/s:
....
....
....
....

Date

Notes

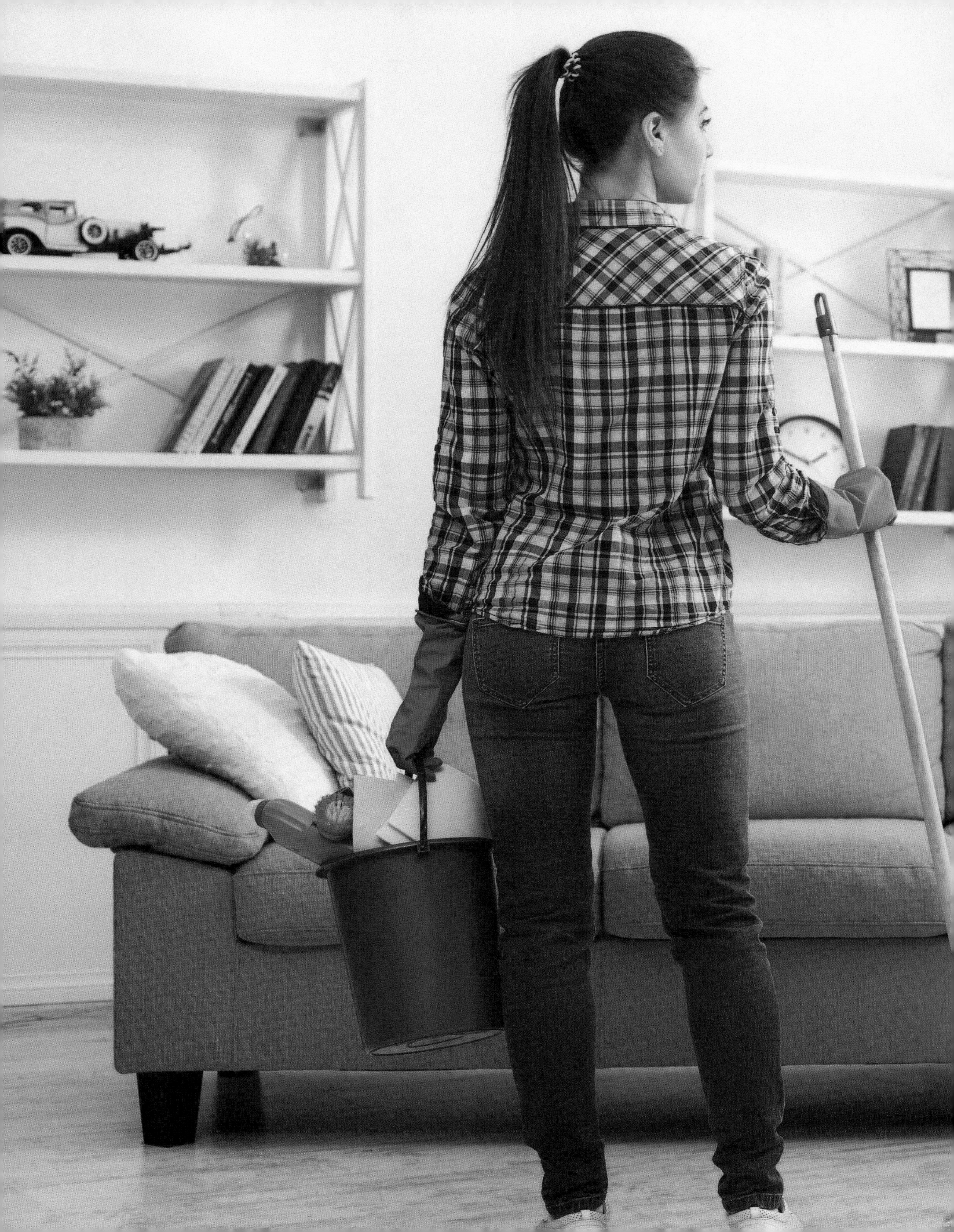

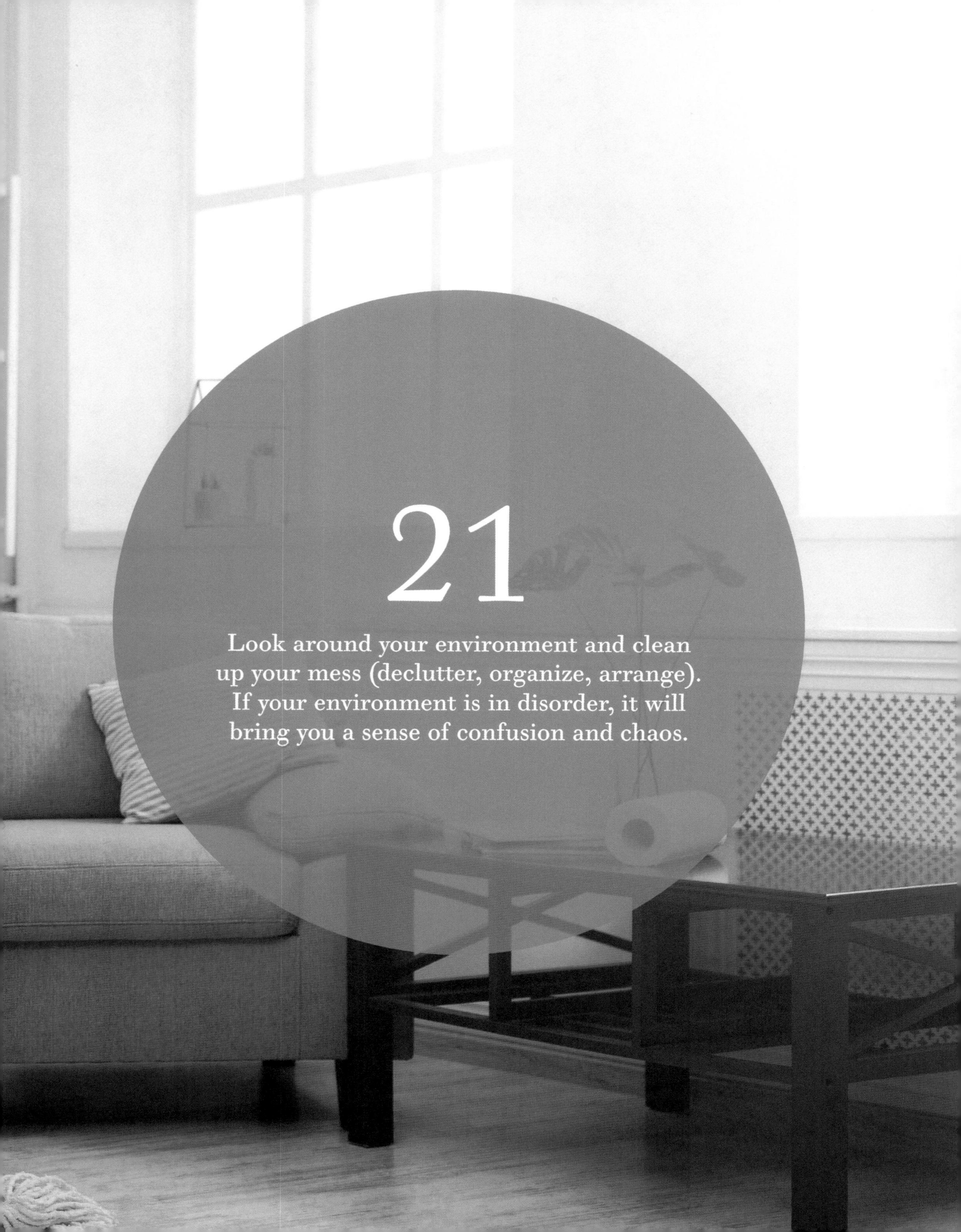

21

Look around your environment and clean up your mess (declutter, organize, arrange). If your environment is in disorder, it will bring you a sense of confusion and chaos.

Date
....

Thought/s:
....
....
....
....

Feeling/s:
....
....
....
....
....

Behavior/s:
....
....
....
....

Goal/s:
....
....
....
....

Date

Notes

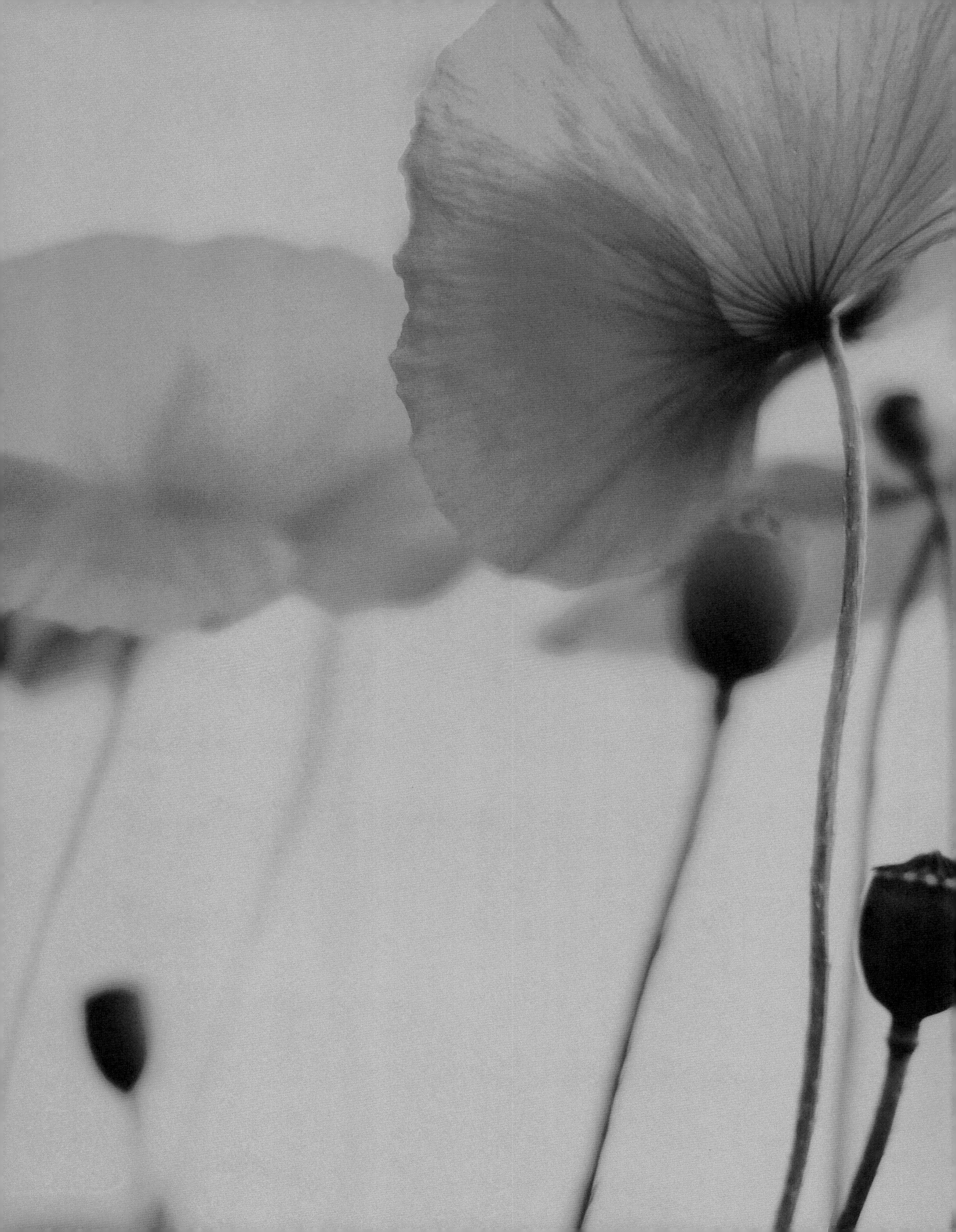

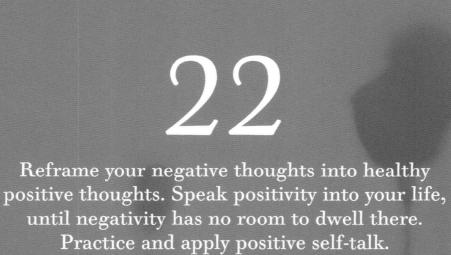

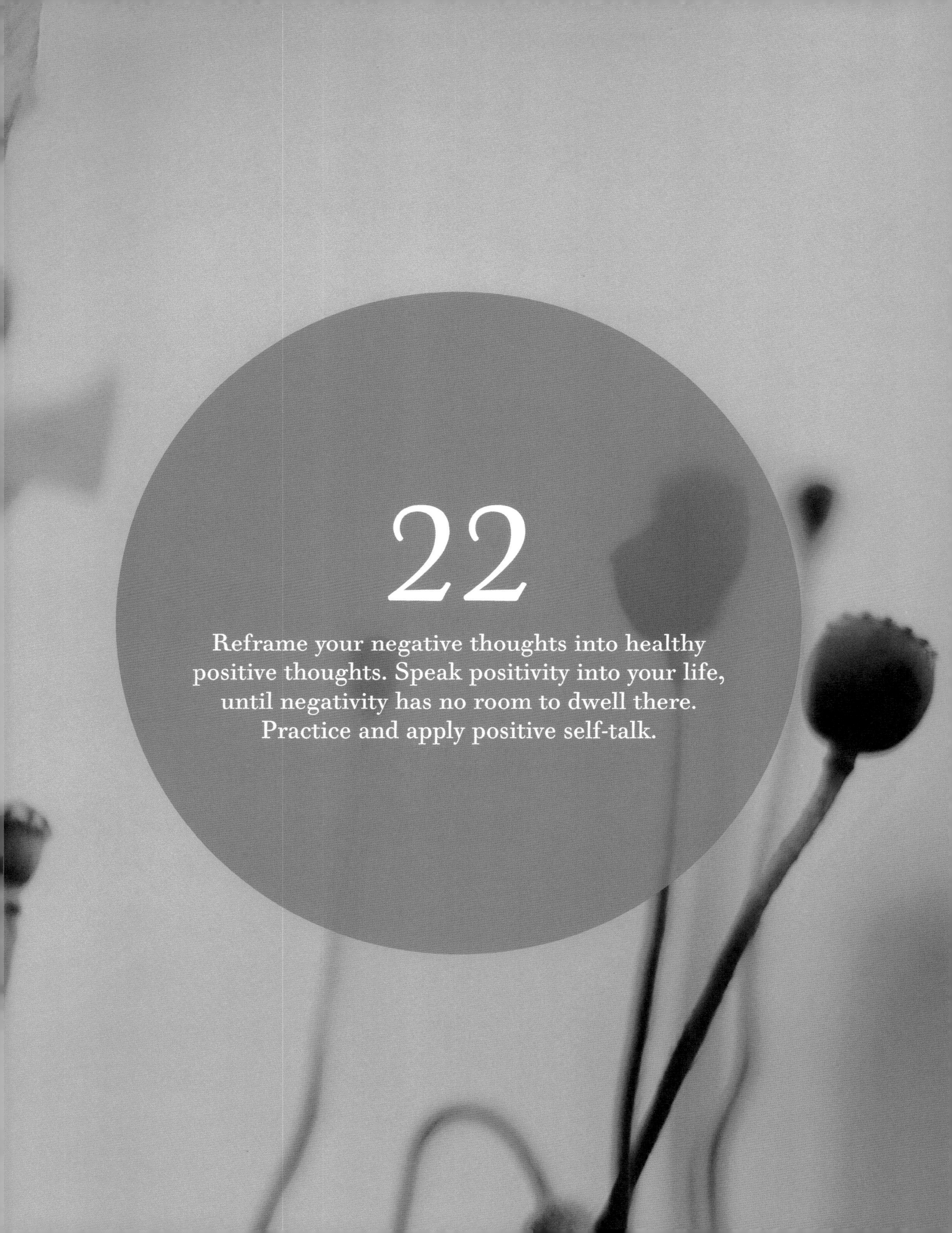

22

Reframe your negative thoughts into healthy positive thoughts. Speak positivity into your life, until negativity has no room to dwell there. Practice and apply positive self-talk.

Date
....

Thought/s:
....
....
....
....

Feeling/s:
....
....
....
....
....

Behavior/s:
....
....
....
....

Goal/s:
....
....
....
....

Date

Notes

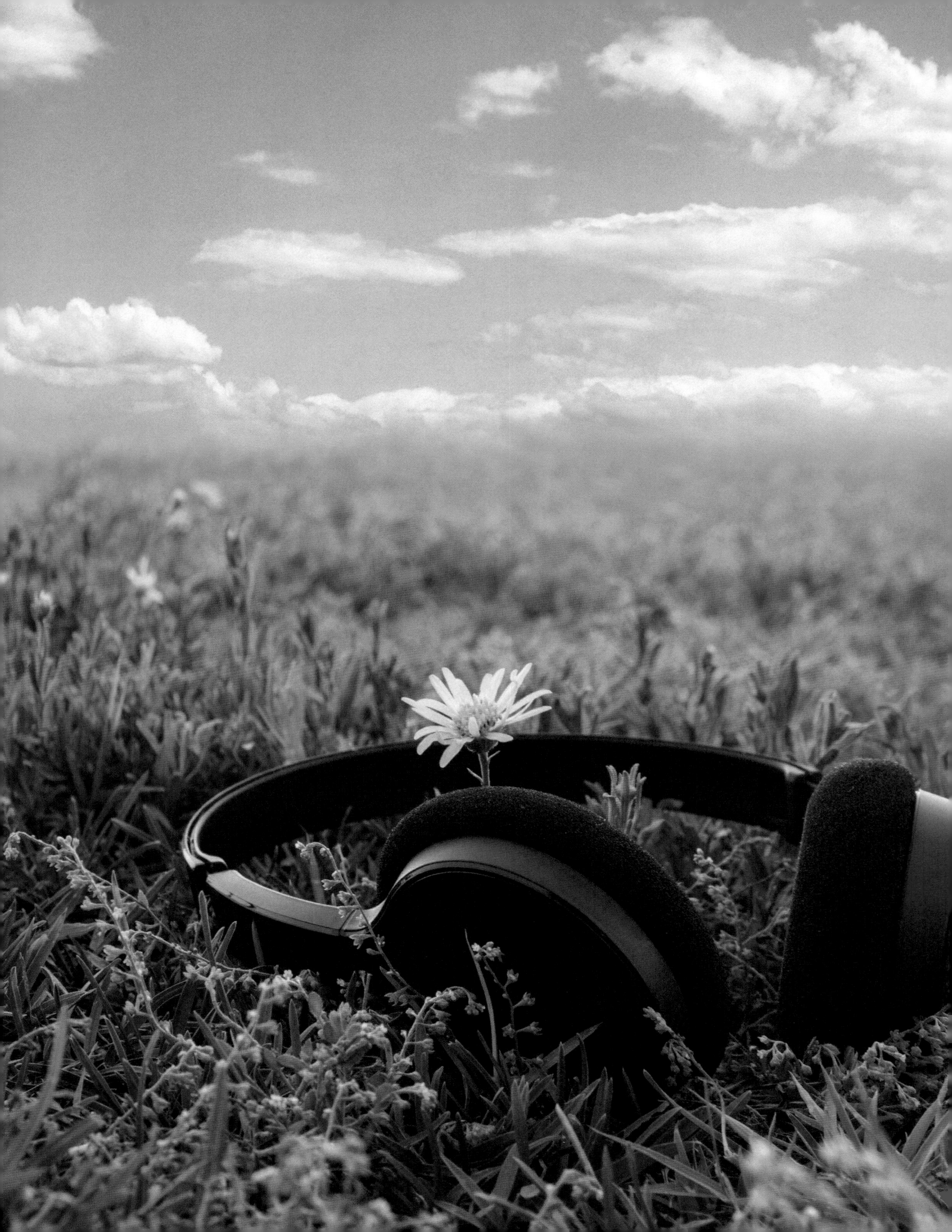

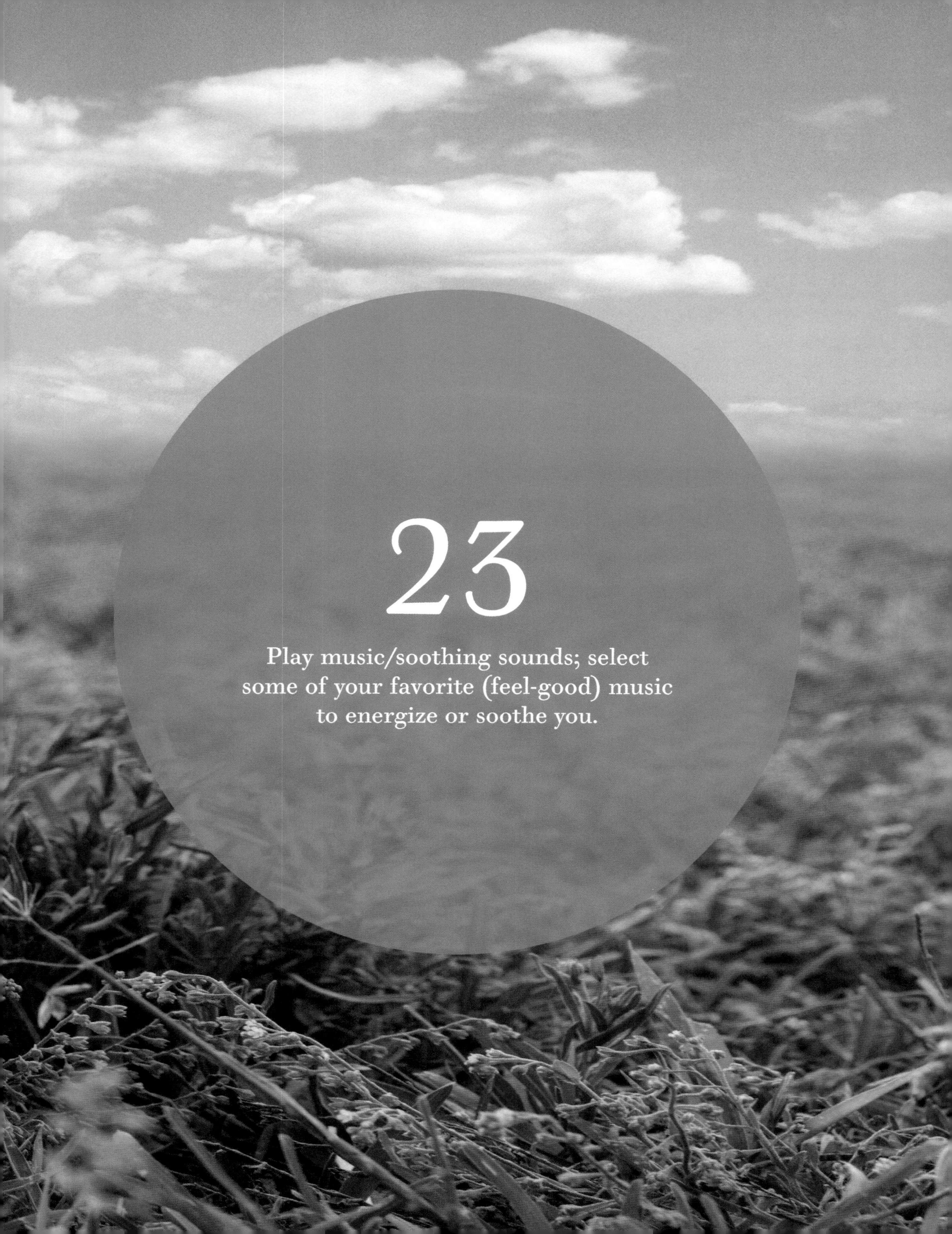

23

Play music/soothing sounds; select some of your favorite (feel-good) music to energize or soothe you.

Date
....

Thought/s:
....
....
....
....

Feeling/s:
....
....
....
....

Behavior/s:
....
....
....
....

Goal/s:
....
....
....
....

Date
....

Notes
....
....
....
....
....
....
....
....
....
....
....
....
....
....
....
....
....

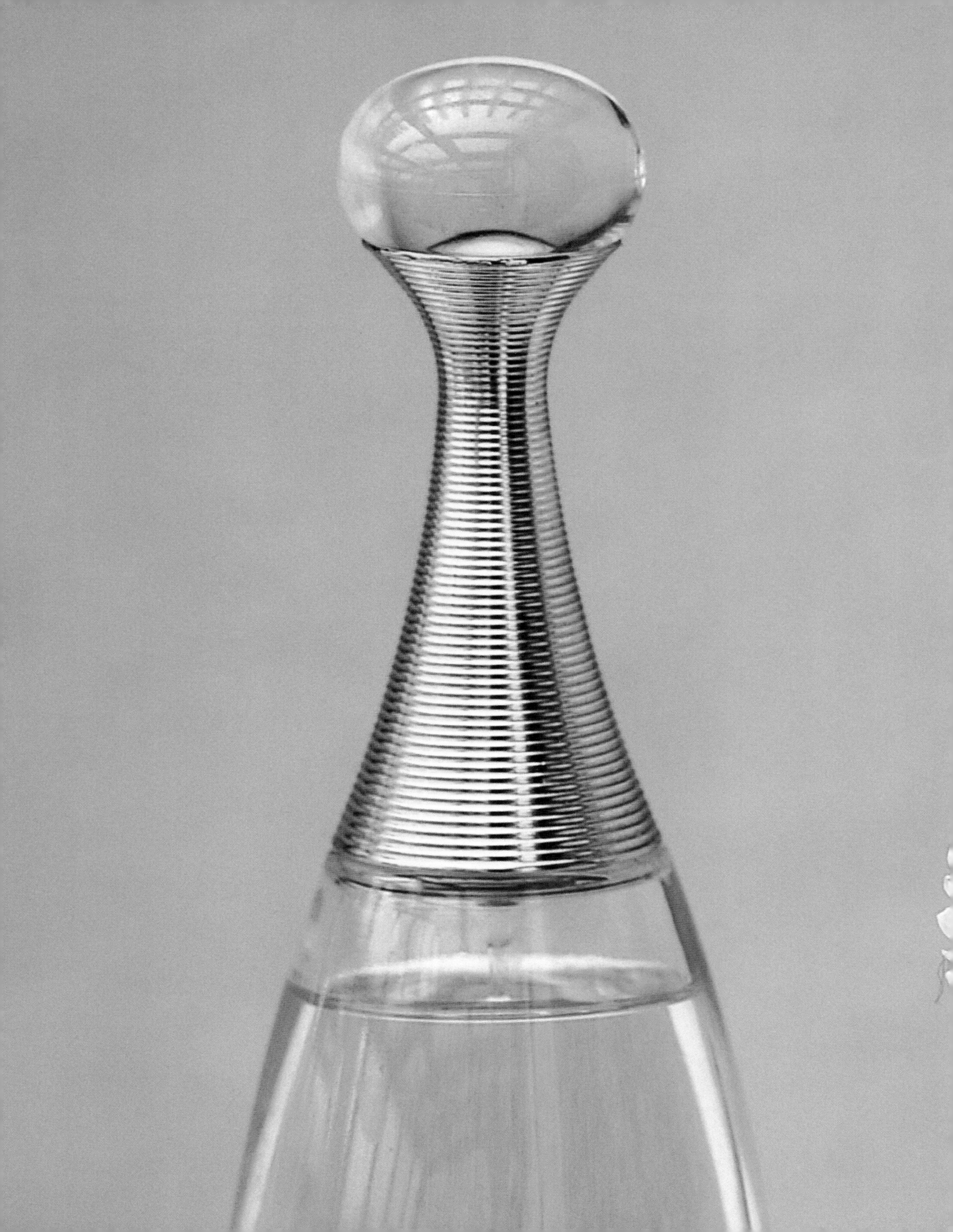

24

Apply pleasant smells to your environment (aromatherapy, scented candle, peppermint, whatever you like).

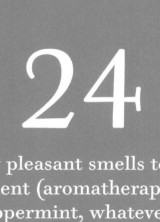

Date
....

Thought/s:
....
....
....
....

Feeling/s:
....
....
....
....
....

Behavior/s:
....
....
....
....

Goal/s:
....
....
....
....

Date
....

Notes
....

....

....

....

....

....

....

....

....

....

....

....

....

....

....

....

....

....

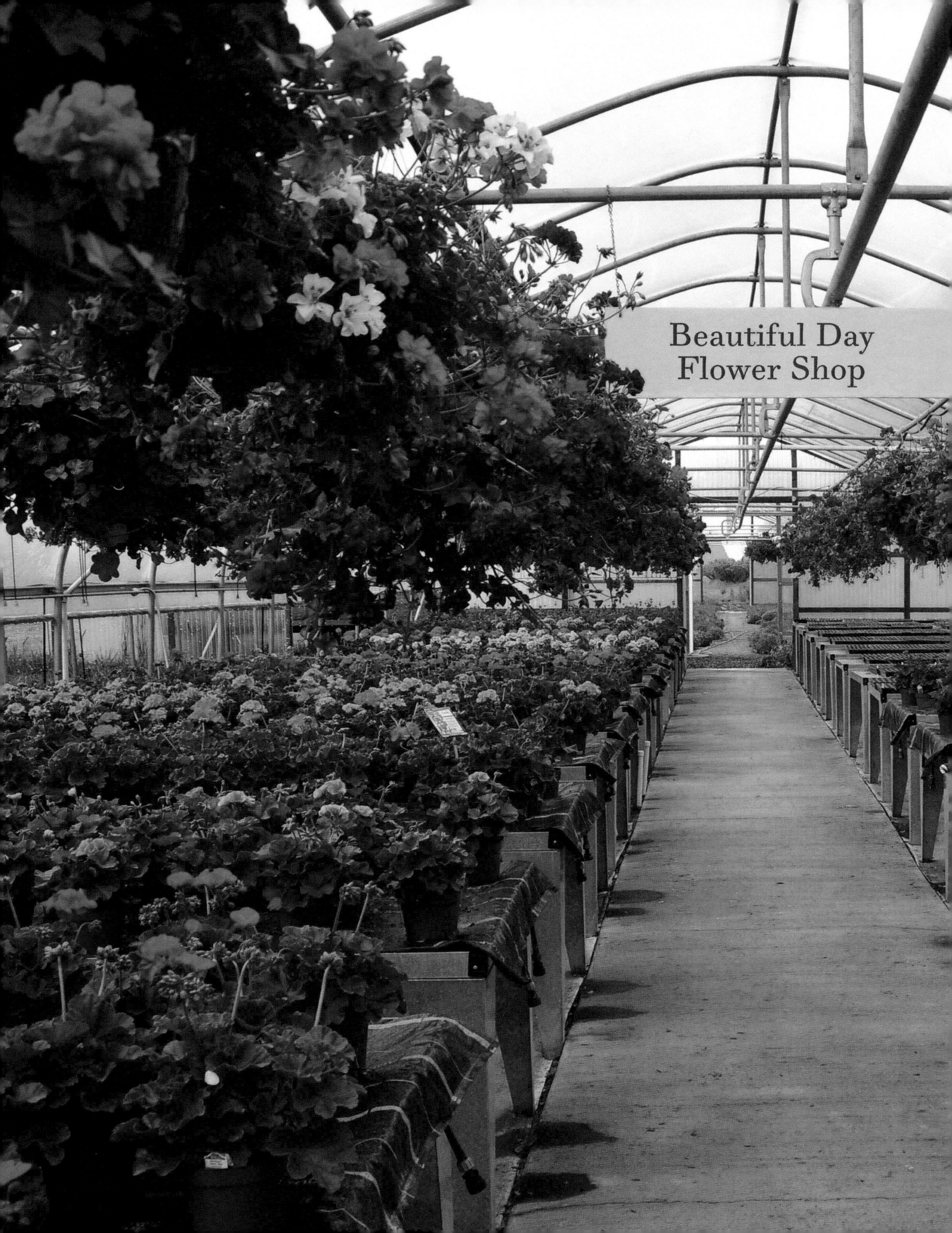
Beautiful Day
Flower Shop

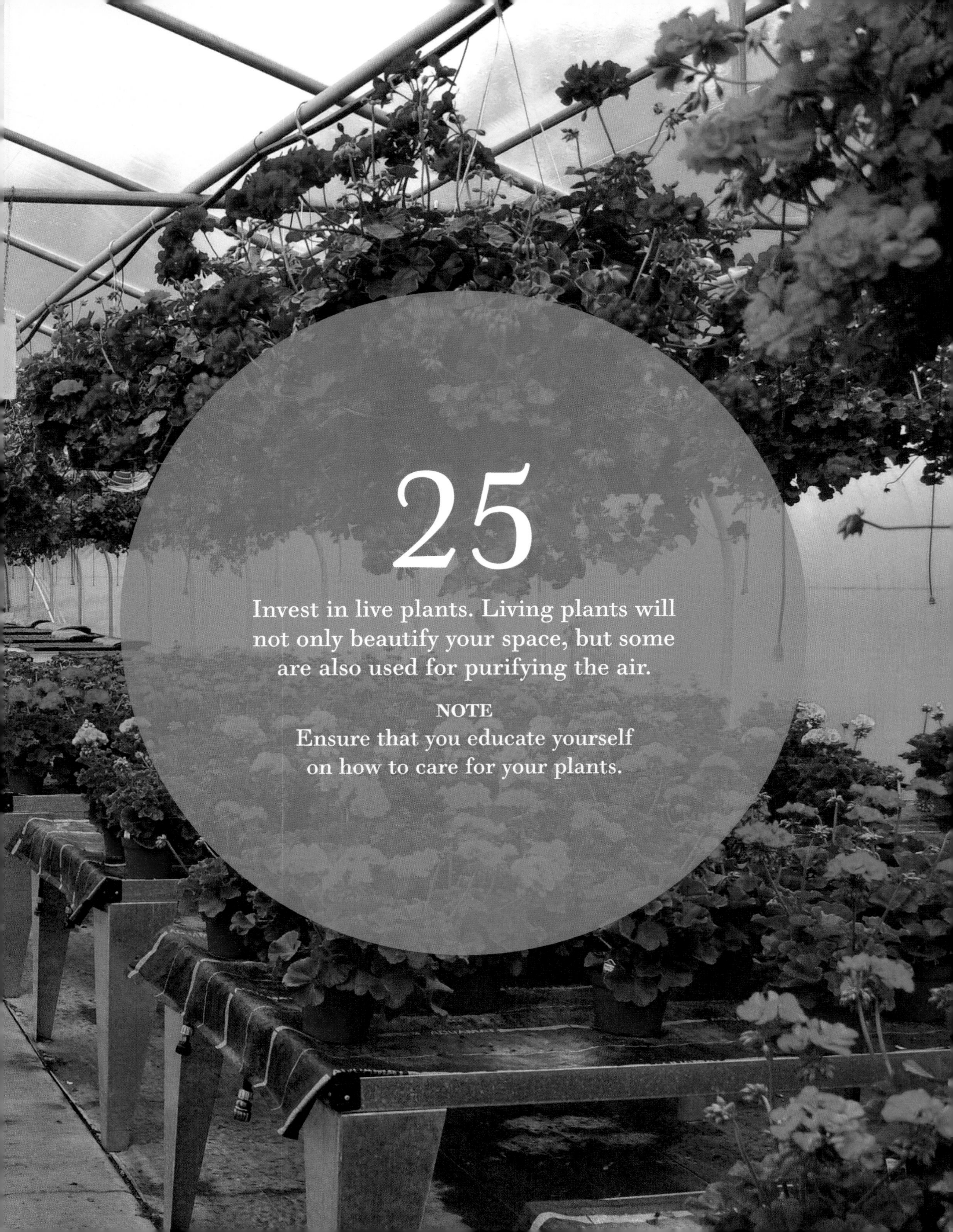

25

Invest in live plants. Living plants will not only beautify your space, but some are also used for purifying the air.

NOTE

Ensure that you educate yourself on how to care for your plants.

Date
....

Thought/s:
....
....
....
....

Feeling/s:
....
....
....
....

Behavior/s:
....
....
....
....

Goal/s:
....
....
....
....

Date
....

Notes
....
....
....
....
....
....
....
....
....
....
....
....
....
....
....
....
....
....

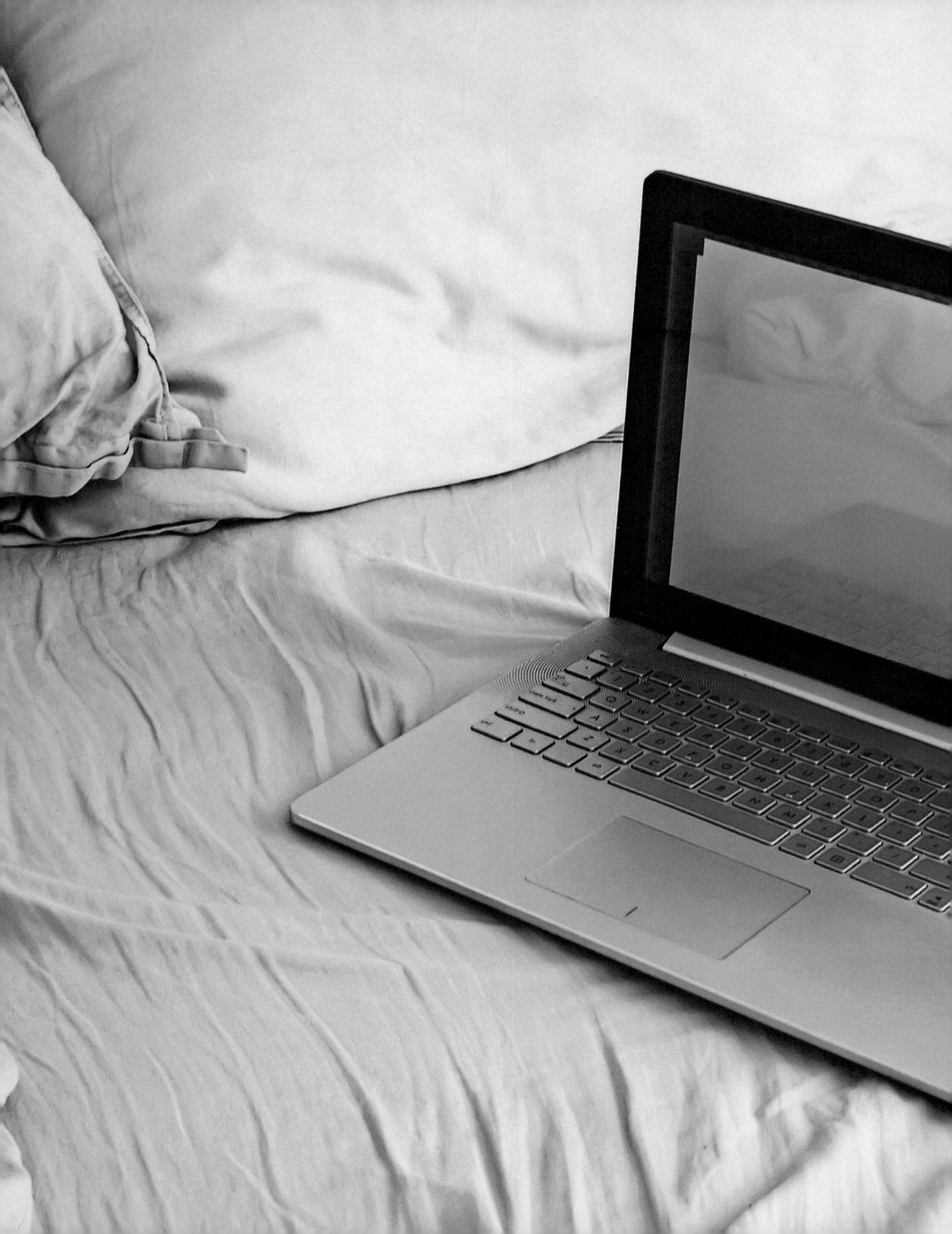

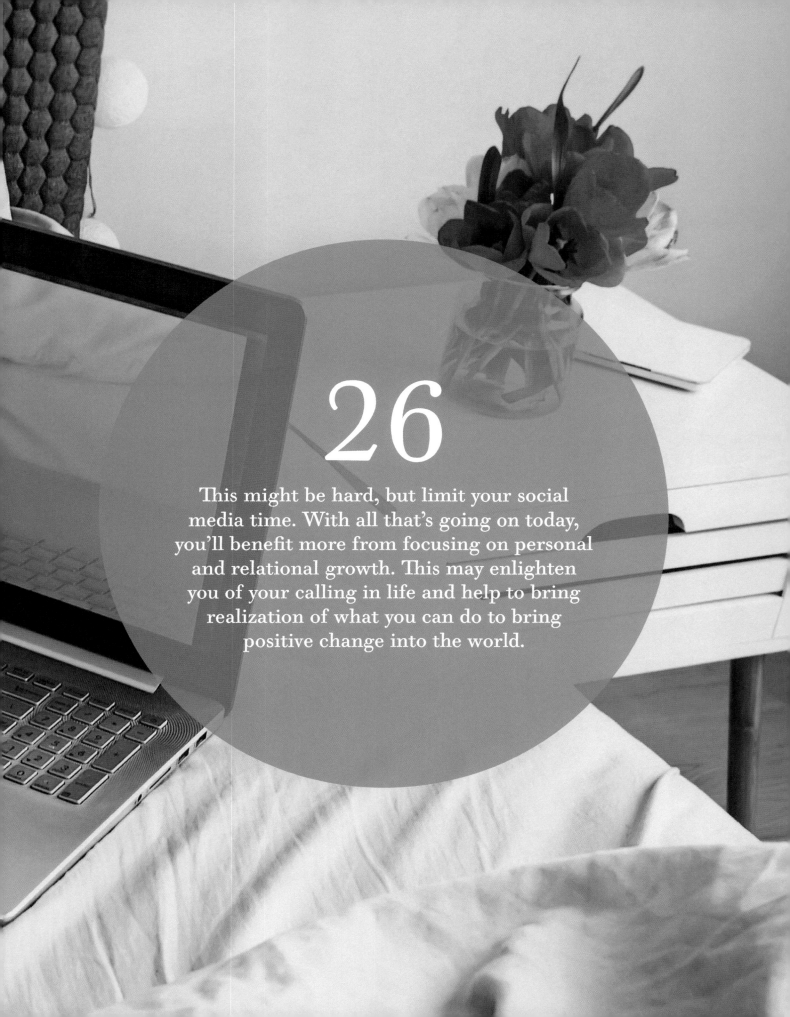

26

This might be hard, but limit your social media time. With all that's going on today, you'll benefit more from focusing on personal and relational growth. This may enlighten you of your calling in life and help to bring realization of what you can do to bring positive change into the world.

Date

....

Thought/s:
....
....
....
....

Feeling/s:
....
....
....
....

Behavior/s:
....
....
....
....

Goal/s:
....
....
....
....

Date

Notes

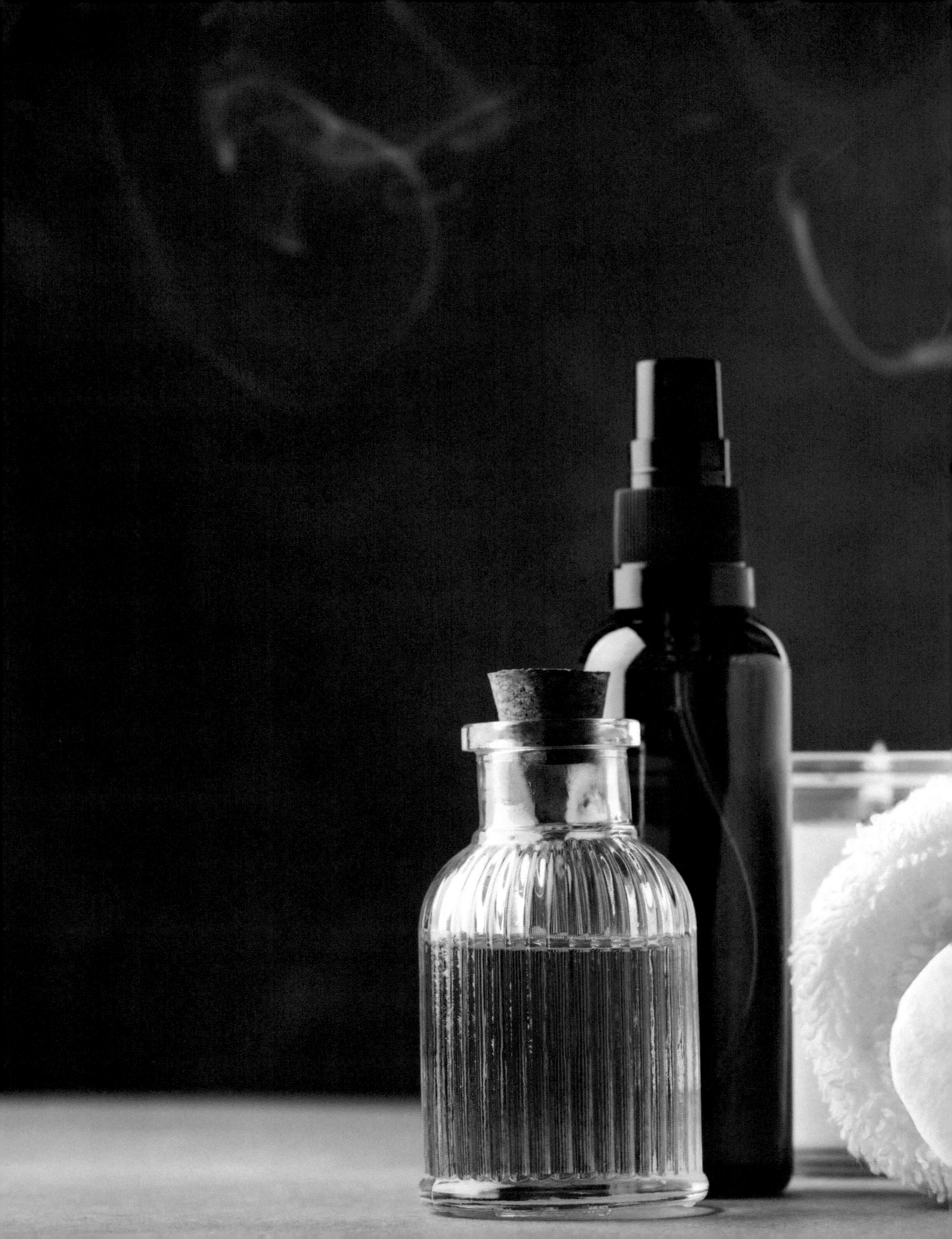

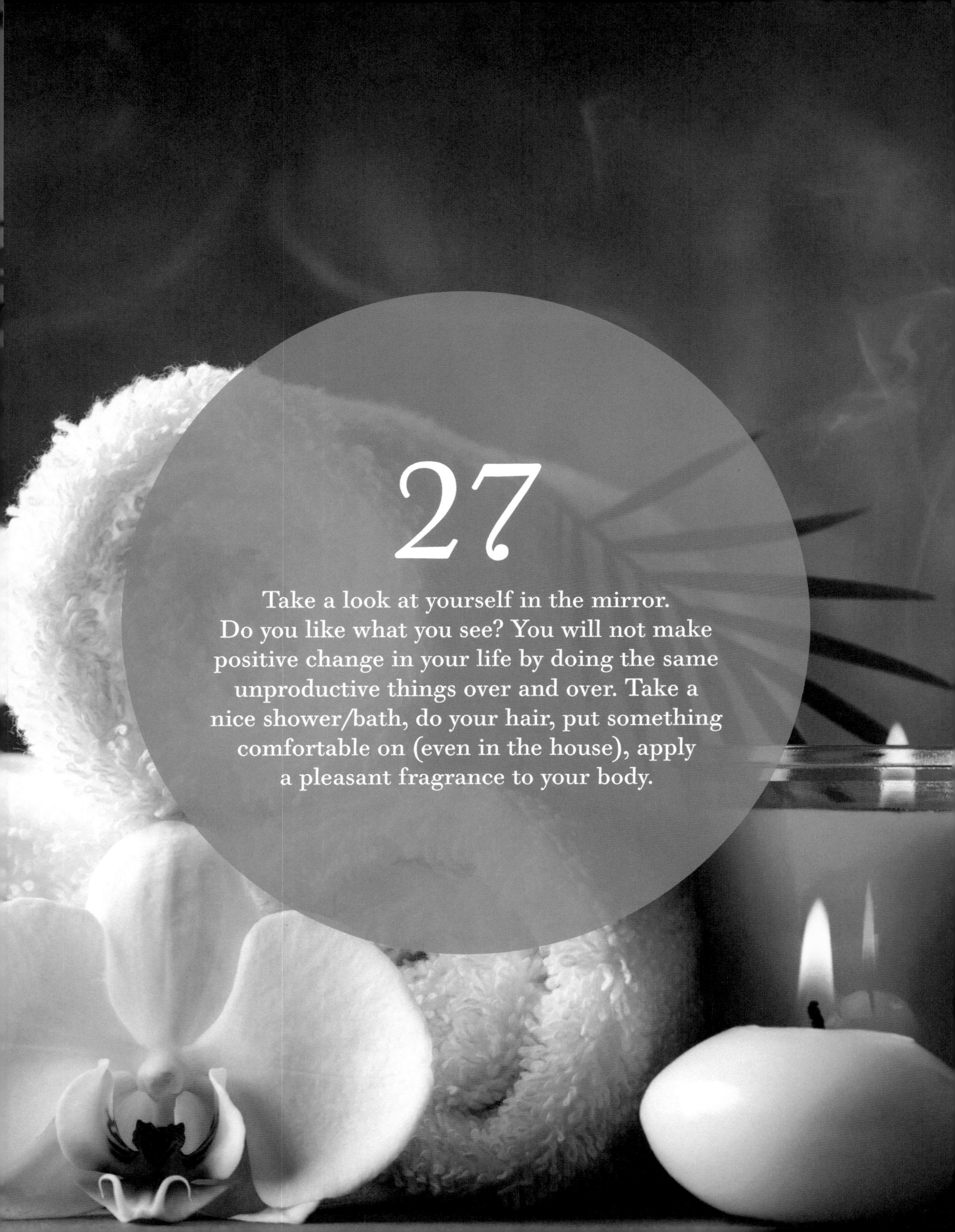

27

Take a look at yourself in the mirror. Do you like what you see? You will not make positive change in your life by doing the same unproductive things over and over. Take a nice shower/bath, do your hair, put something comfortable on (even in the house), apply a pleasant fragrance to your body.

Date
....

Thought/s:
....
....
....
....

Feeling/s:
....
....
....
....

Behavior/s:
....
....
....
....

Goal/s:
....
....
....
....

Date

Notes

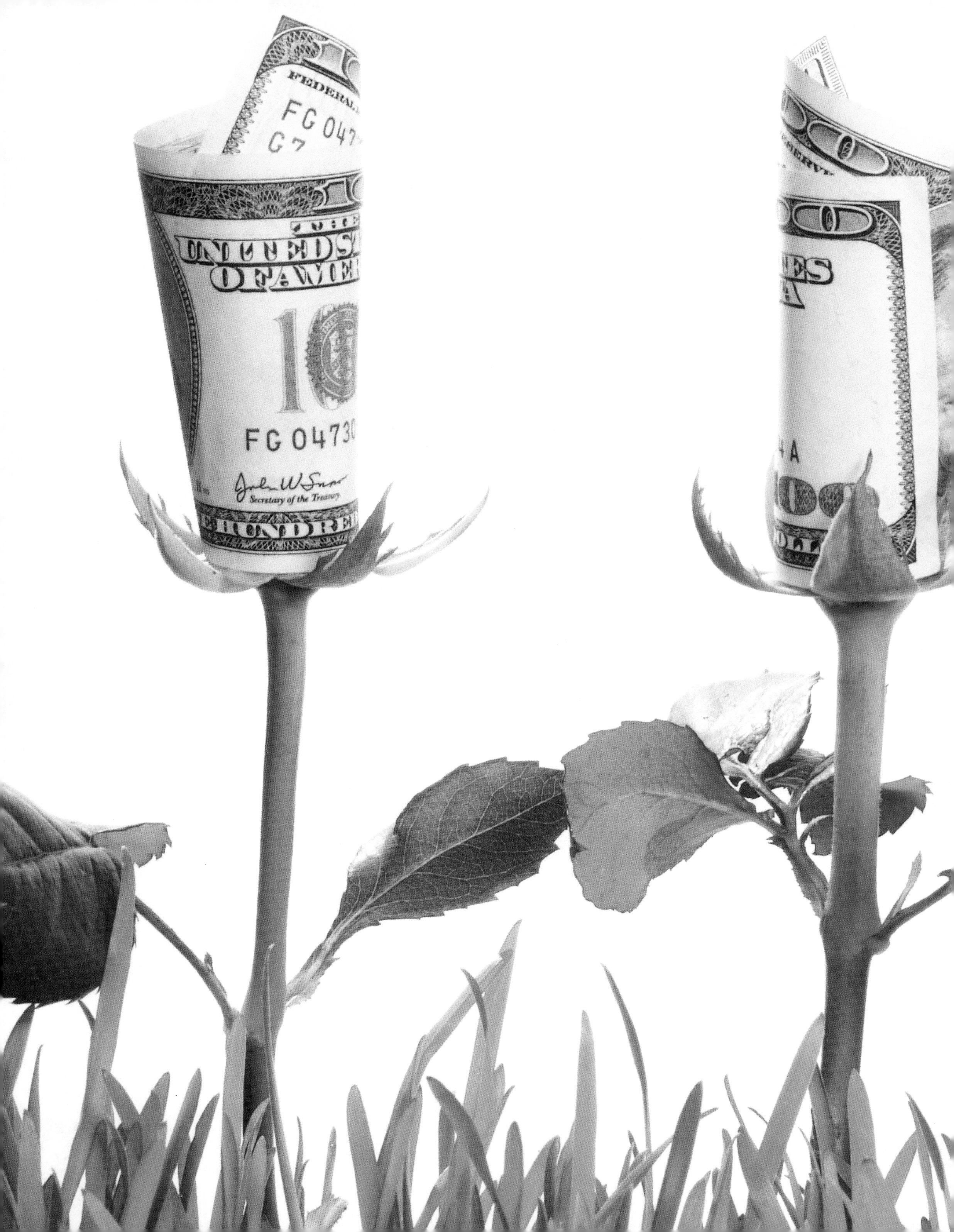
FG04730
Secretary of the Treasury.

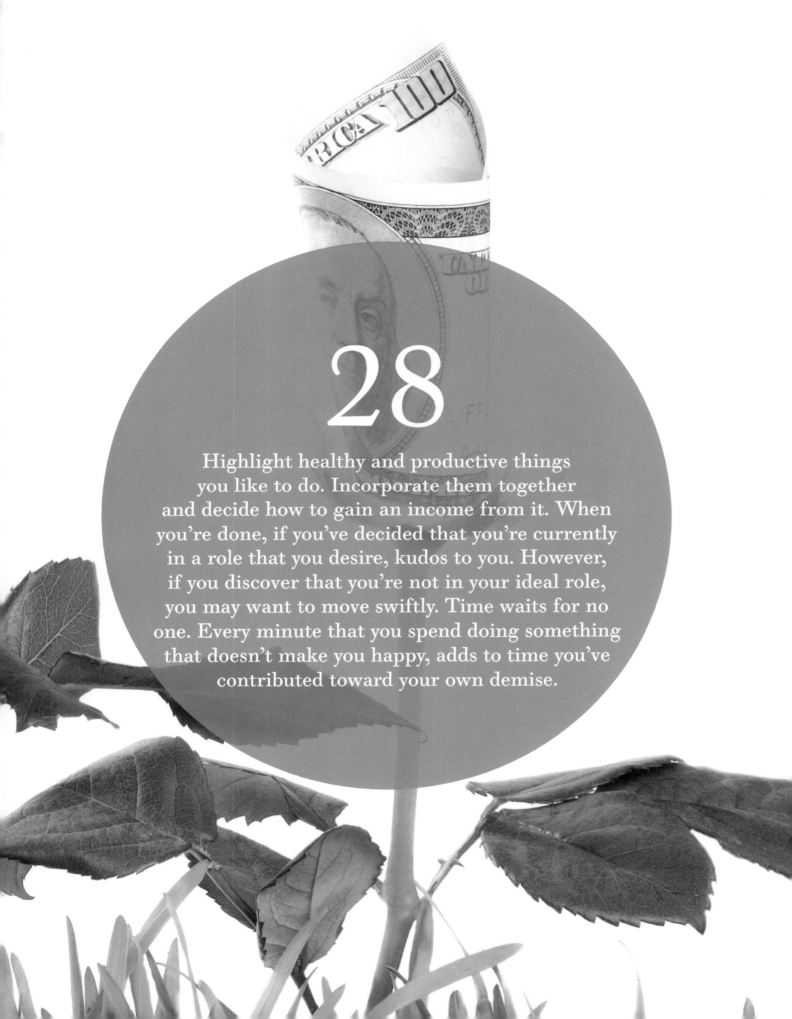

28

Highlight healthy and productive things you like to do. Incorporate them together and decide how to gain an income from it. When you're done, if you've decided that you're currently in a role that you desire, kudos to you. However, if you discover that you're not in your ideal role, you may want to move swiftly. Time waits for no one. Every minute that you spend doing something that doesn't make you happy, adds to time you've contributed toward your own demise.

Date
....

Thought/s:
....
....
....
....

Feeling/s:
....
....
....
....

Behavior/s:
....
....
....
....

Goal/s:
....
....
....
....

Date

Notes

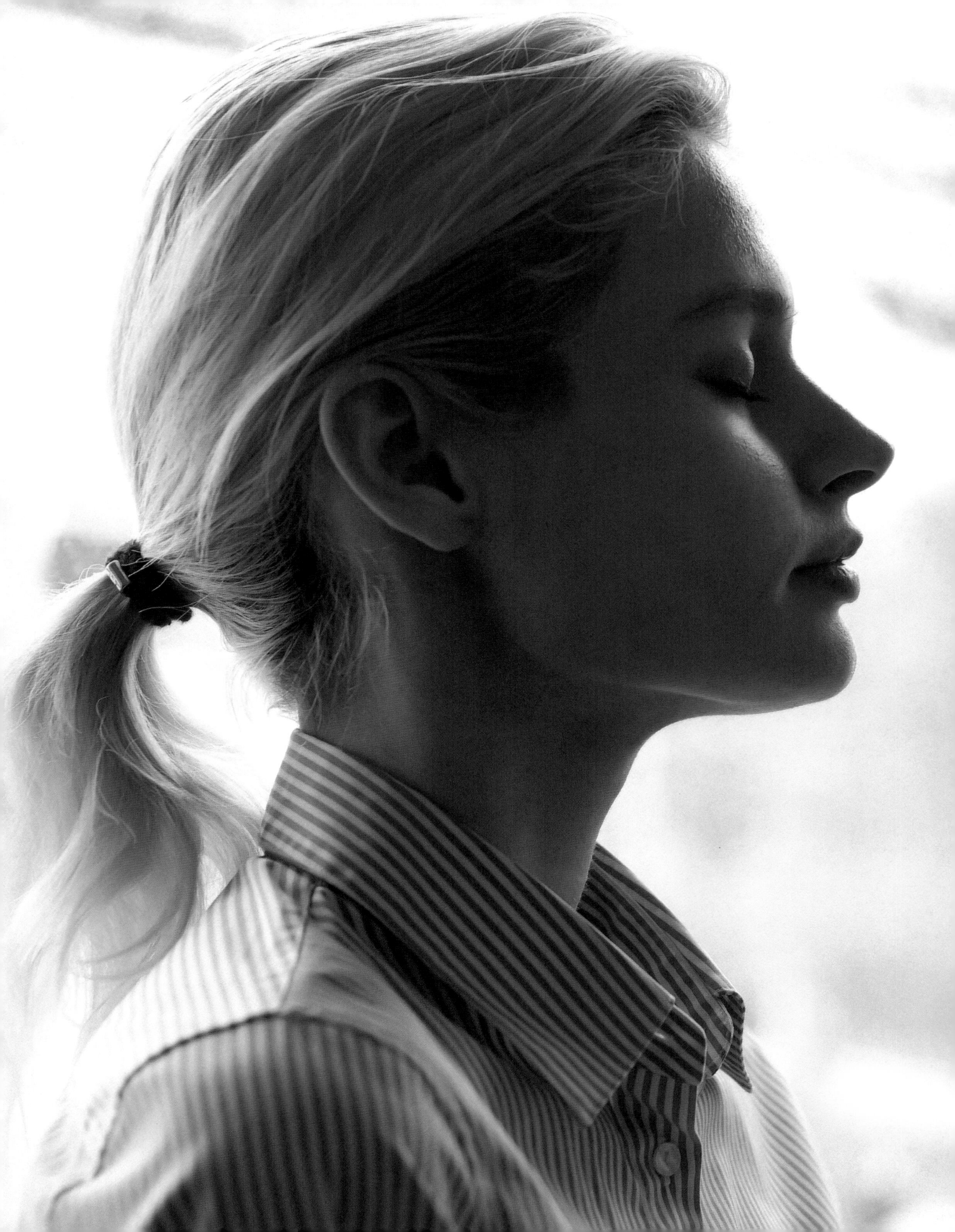

29

Implement deep breathing exercises and reflection. Identify a safe, peaceful place to devote a minimum of five minutes (by yourself) for quiet time. During this time, you should clear your mind of all things. Close your eyes and leave yourself vulnerable to the utilization of your five sense. Yes, even your sight, although your eyes are closed.

Date
....

Thought/s:
....
....
....
....

Feeling/s:
....
....
....
....

Behavior/s:
....
....
....
....

Goal/s:
....
....
....
....

Date

Notes

le

y to

ugh

wrap

a

a

c

ary

r Jo´-ses

CHAPT

The resurr

AND ʳ when the sabba
Mag´-da-lene, and
of James, and Sa-lo´-
sweet spices, that they
anoint him.

2 ʳ And very early in the
day of the week, they
sepulcher at the rising of

3 And they said among
shall roll us away the st

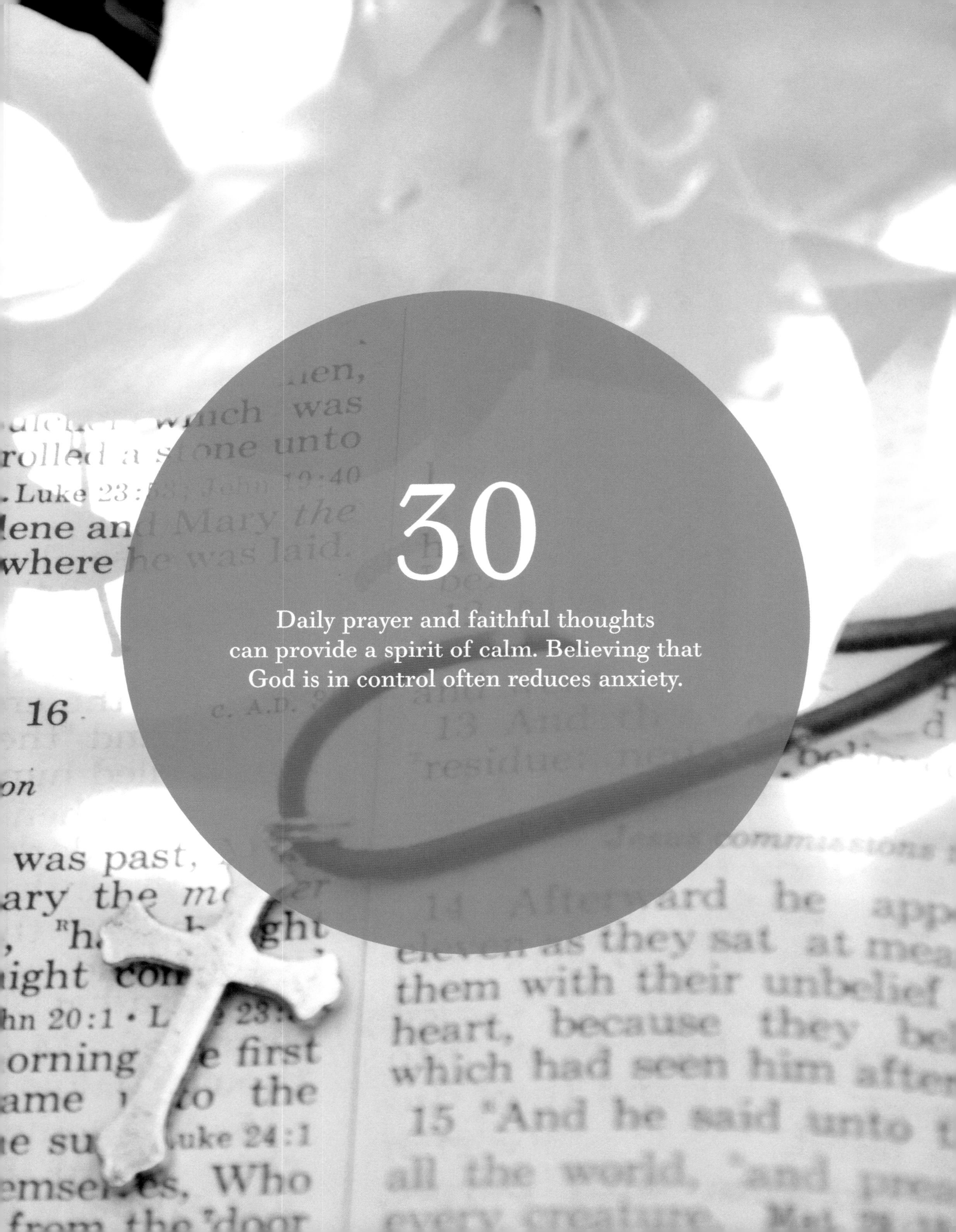

30

Daily prayer and faithful thoughts can provide a spirit of calm. Believing that God is in control often reduces anxiety.

Date ....

Thought/s:
....
....
....
....

Feeling/s:
....
....
....
....

Behavior/s:
....
....
....
....

Goal/s:
....
....
....
....

Date

Notes

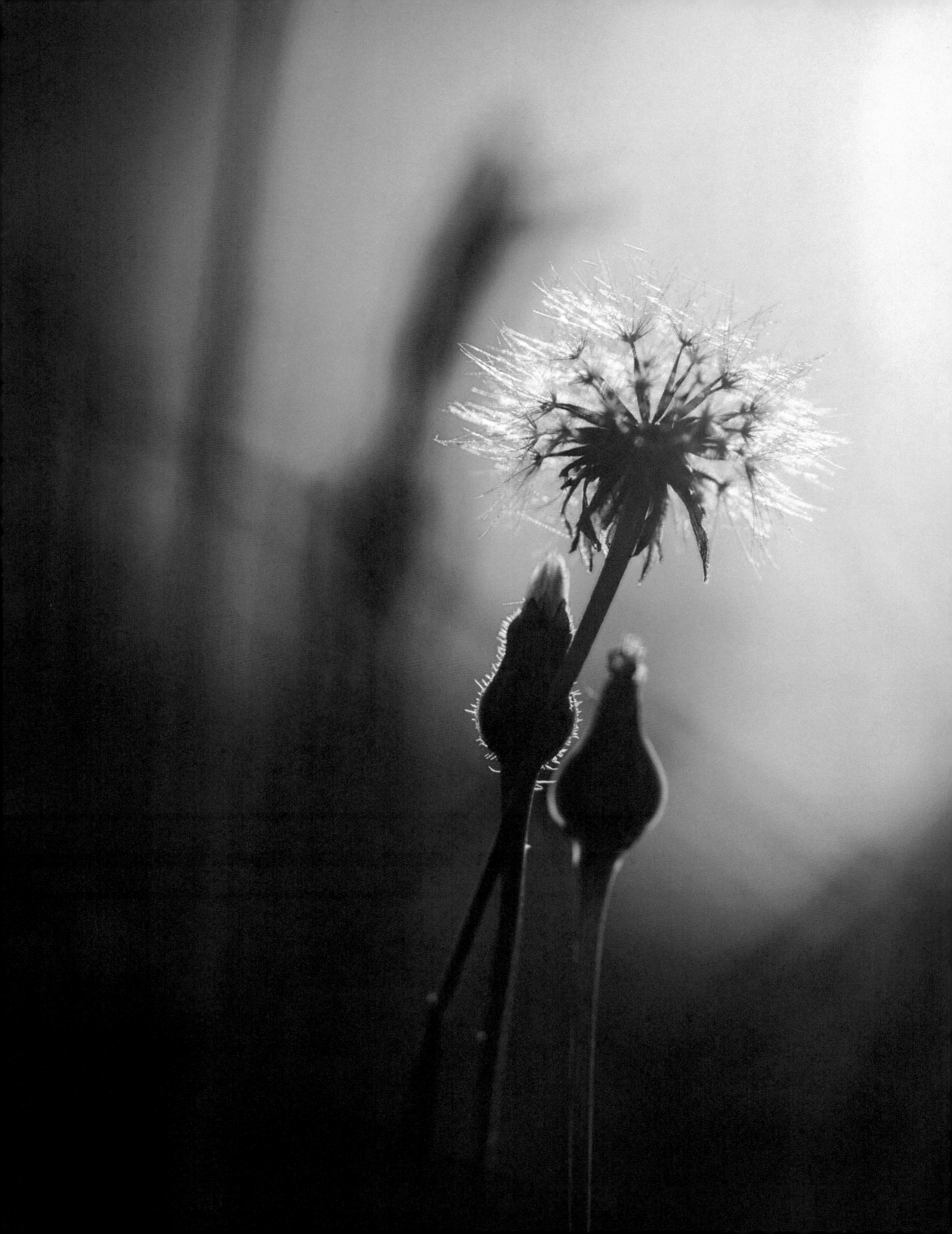

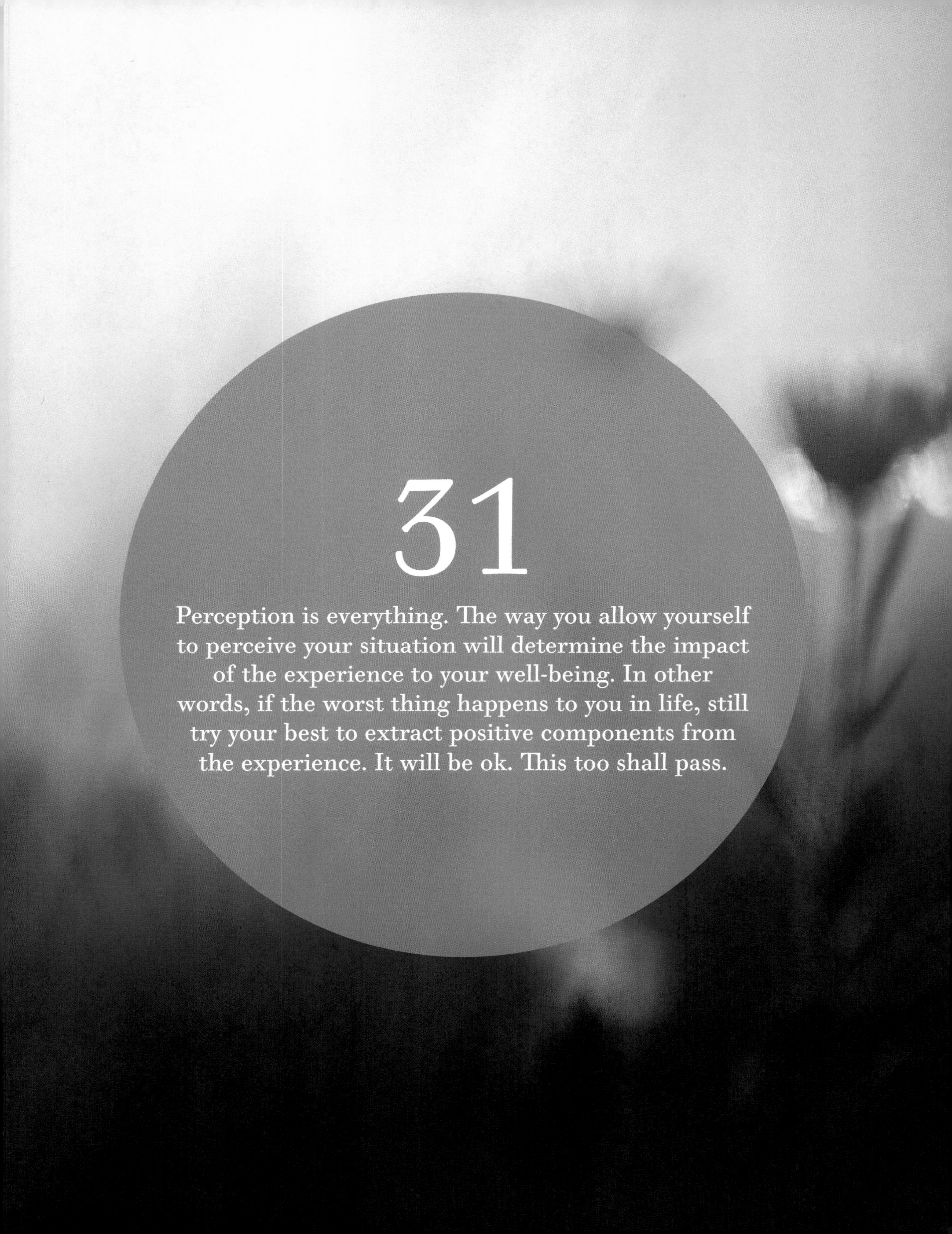

31

Perception is everything. The way you allow yourself to perceive your situation will determine the impact of the experience to your well-being. In other words, if the worst thing happens to you in life, still try your best to extract positive components from the experience. It will be ok. This too shall pass.

Date
....

Thought/s:
....
....
....
....

Feeling/s:
....
....
....
....

Behavior/s:
....
....
....
....

Goal/s:
....
....
....
....

Date

Notes

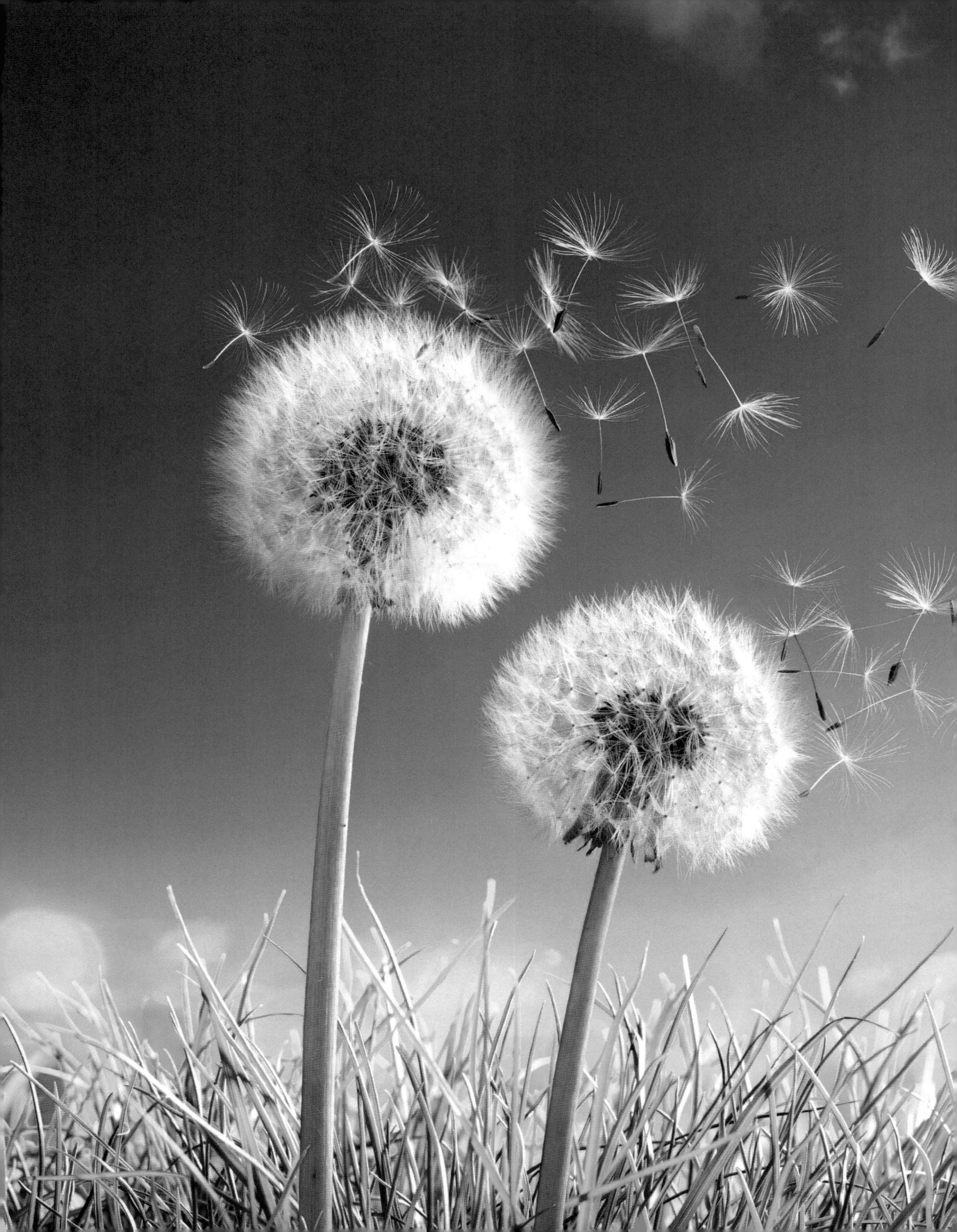

32

Allow your test to become your testimony.
Allow your mess to structure your message.
Allow your storm to build your story.

Date
....

Thought/s:
....
....
....
....

Feeling/s:
....
....
....
....

Behavior/s:
....
....
....
....

Goal/s:
....
....
....
....

Date

Notes

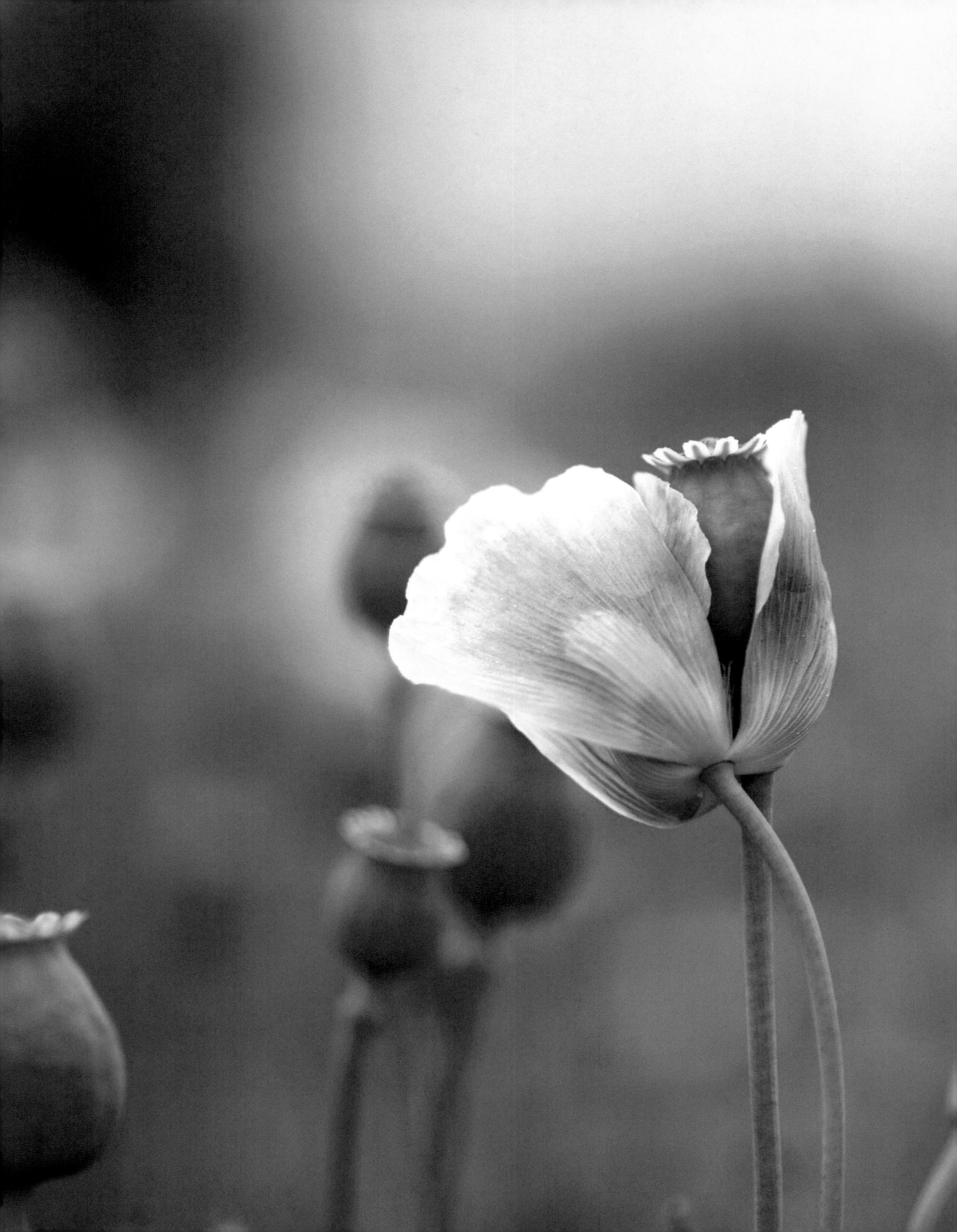

33

Give all that you can give when you can.
Do the best you can when you're in the moment.
This will allow little room for regret.

Date
....

Thought/s:
....
....
....
....

Feeling/s:
....
....
....
....

Behavior/s:
....
....
....
....

Goal/s:
....
....
....
....

Date ....

Notes
....
....
....
....
....
....
....
....
....
....
....
....
....
....
....
....
....
....

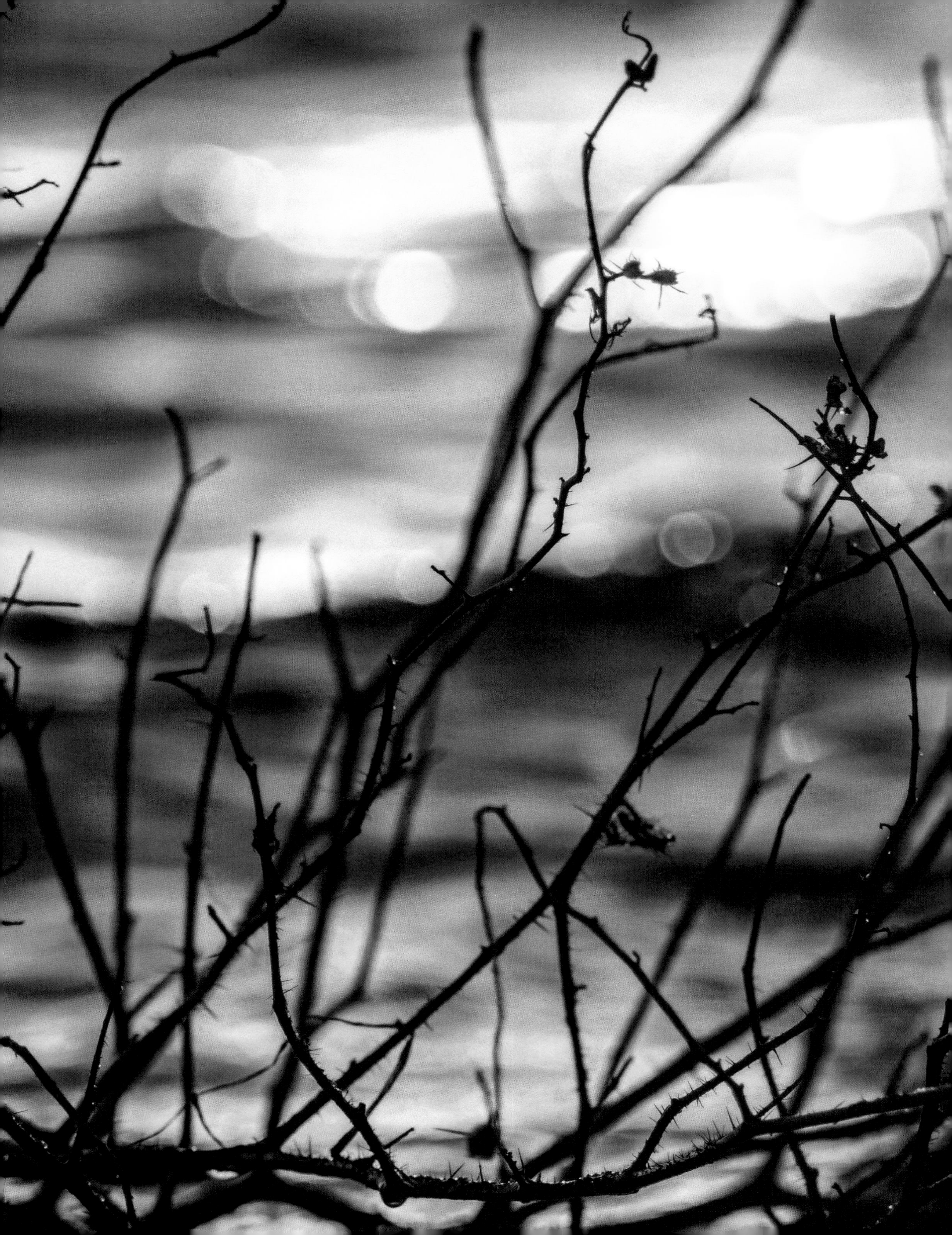

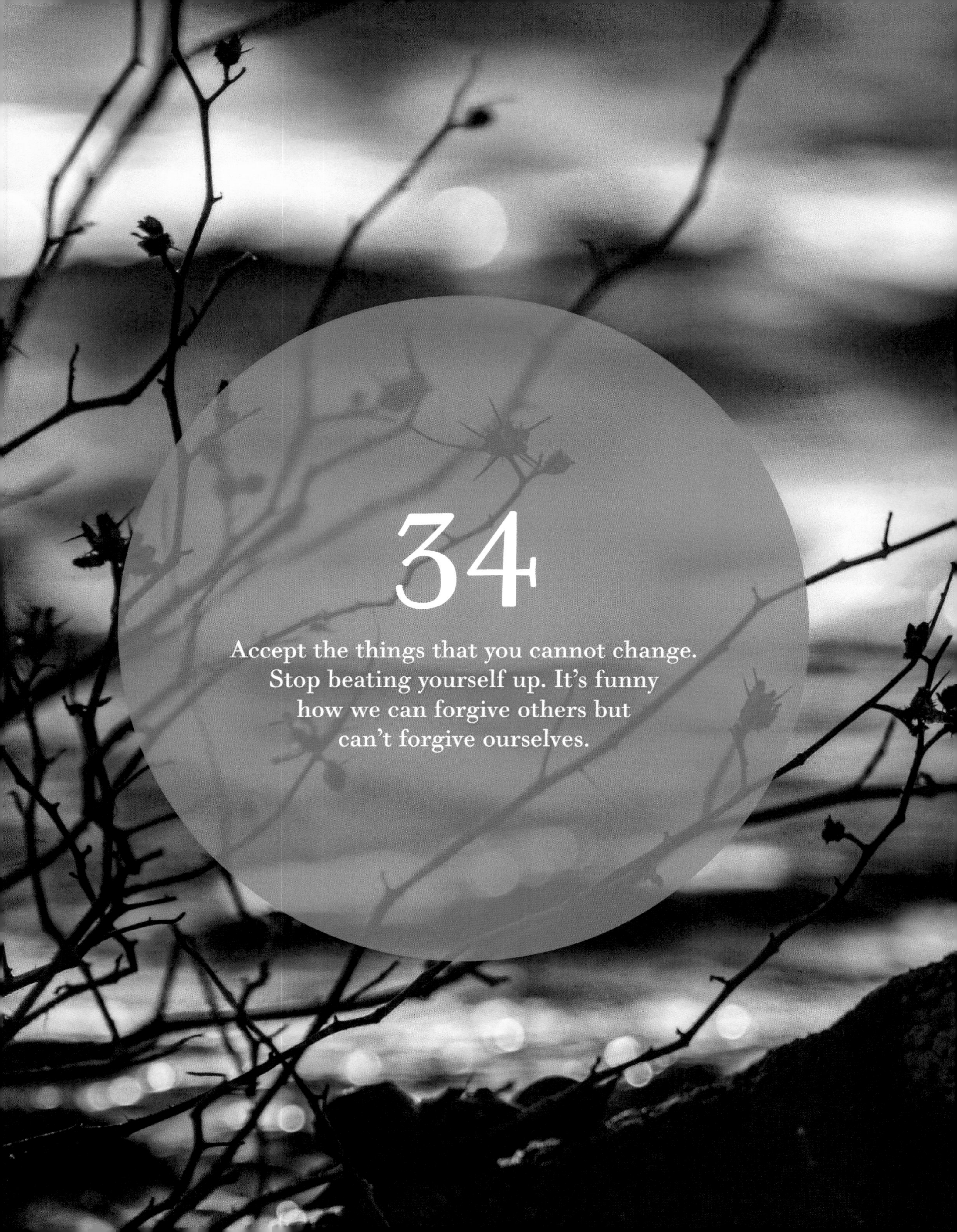

34

Accept the things that you cannot change.
Stop beating yourself up. It's funny
how we can forgive others but
can't forgive ourselves.

Date ....

Thought/s:
....
....
....
....

Feeling/s:
....
....
....
....

Behavior/s:
....
....
....
....

Goal/s:
....
....
....
....

Date

Notes

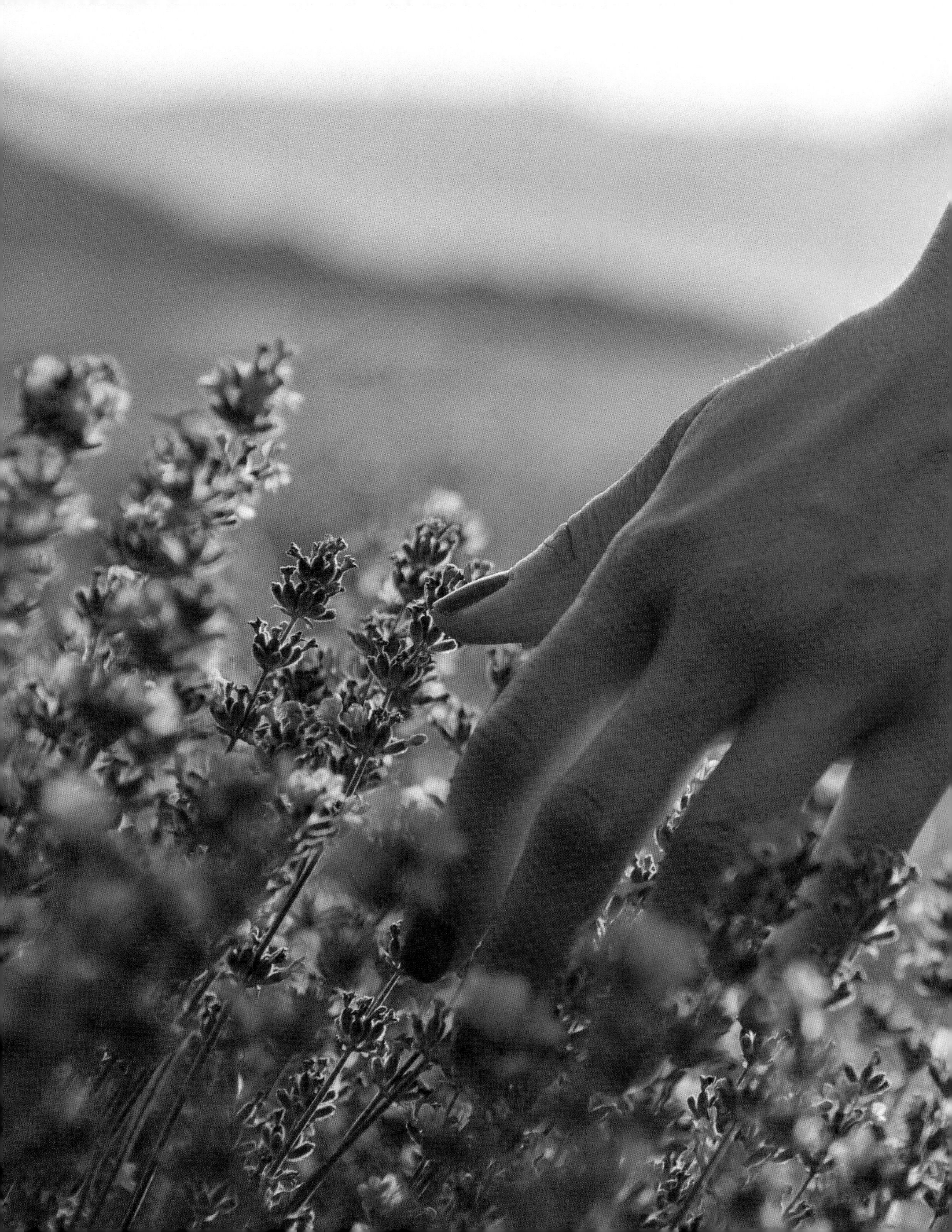

35

Apply introspection and self-awareness prior to apologizing to others. There is a reason why we do what we do. The views, thoughts and behaviors that we have may not always be justified. However, they're our own, and we owe it to ourselves to explore and defend them when necessary.

Date
....

Thought/s:
....
....
....
....

Feeling/s:
....
....
....
....

Behavior/s:
....
....
....
....

Goal/s:
....
....
....
....

Date

Notes

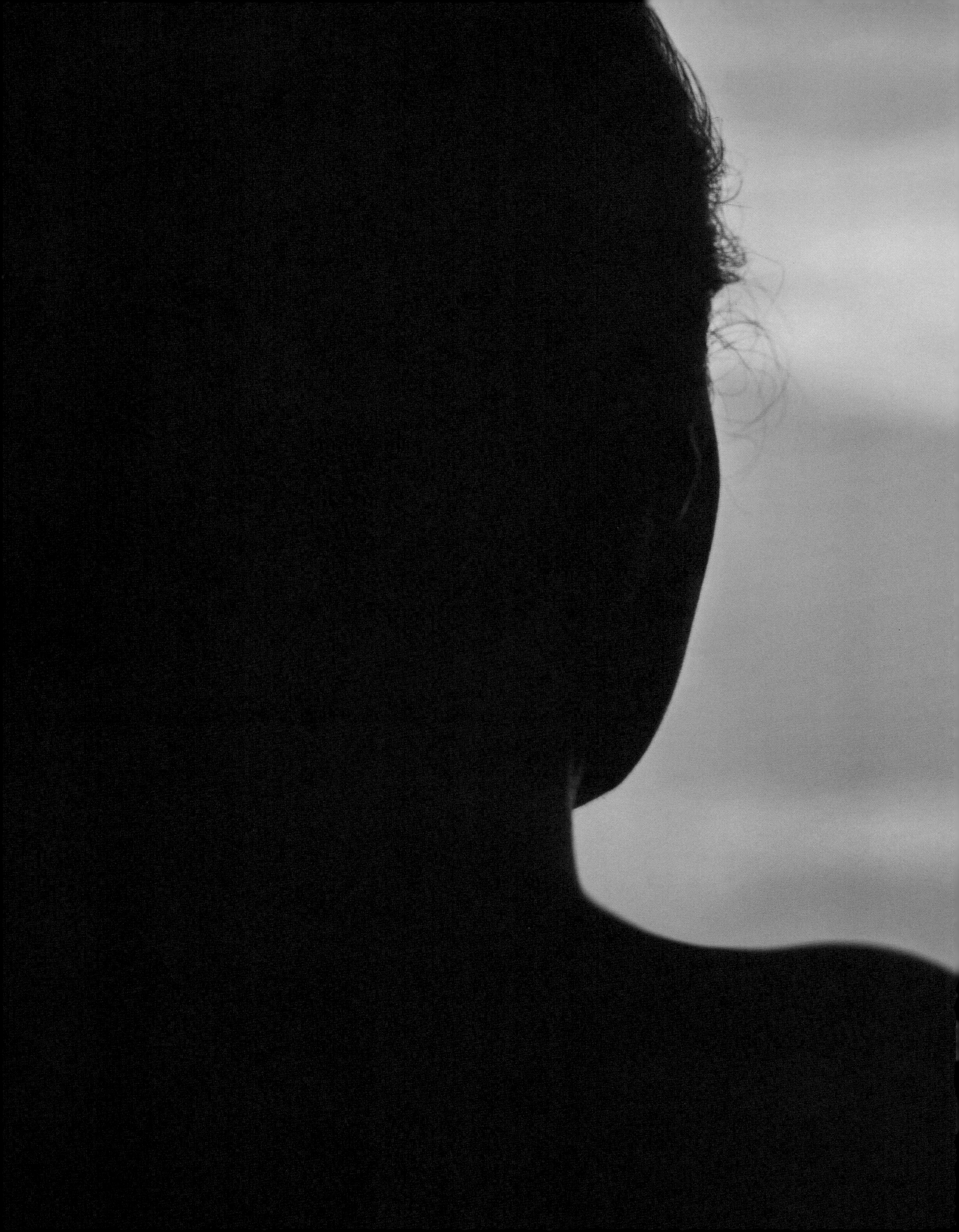

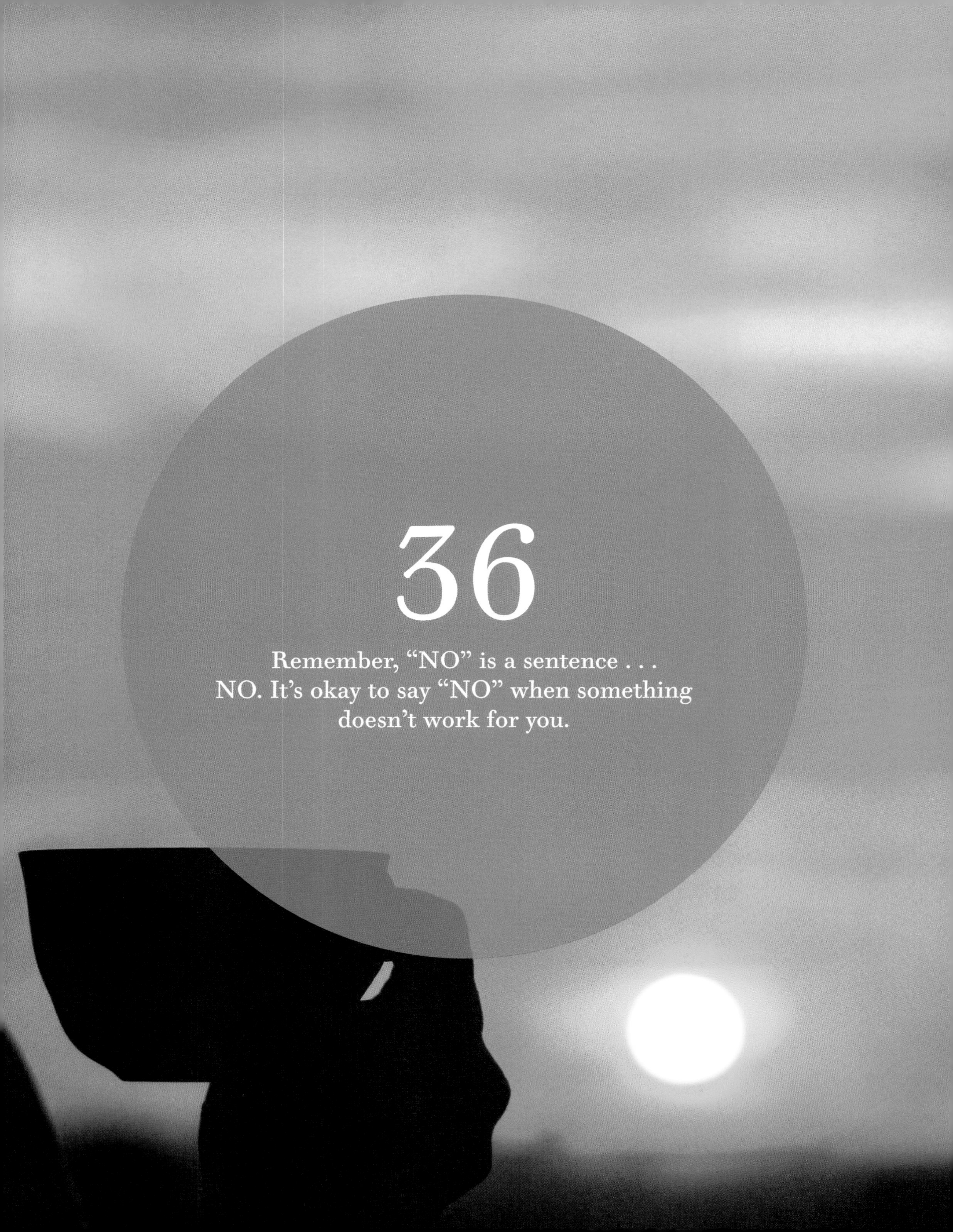

36

Remember, "NO" is a sentence . . .
NO. It's okay to say "NO" when something doesn't work for you.

Date
....

Thought/s:
....
....
....
....

Feeling/s:
....
....
....
....

Behavior/s:
....
....
....
....

Goal/s:
....
....
....
....

Date

Notes

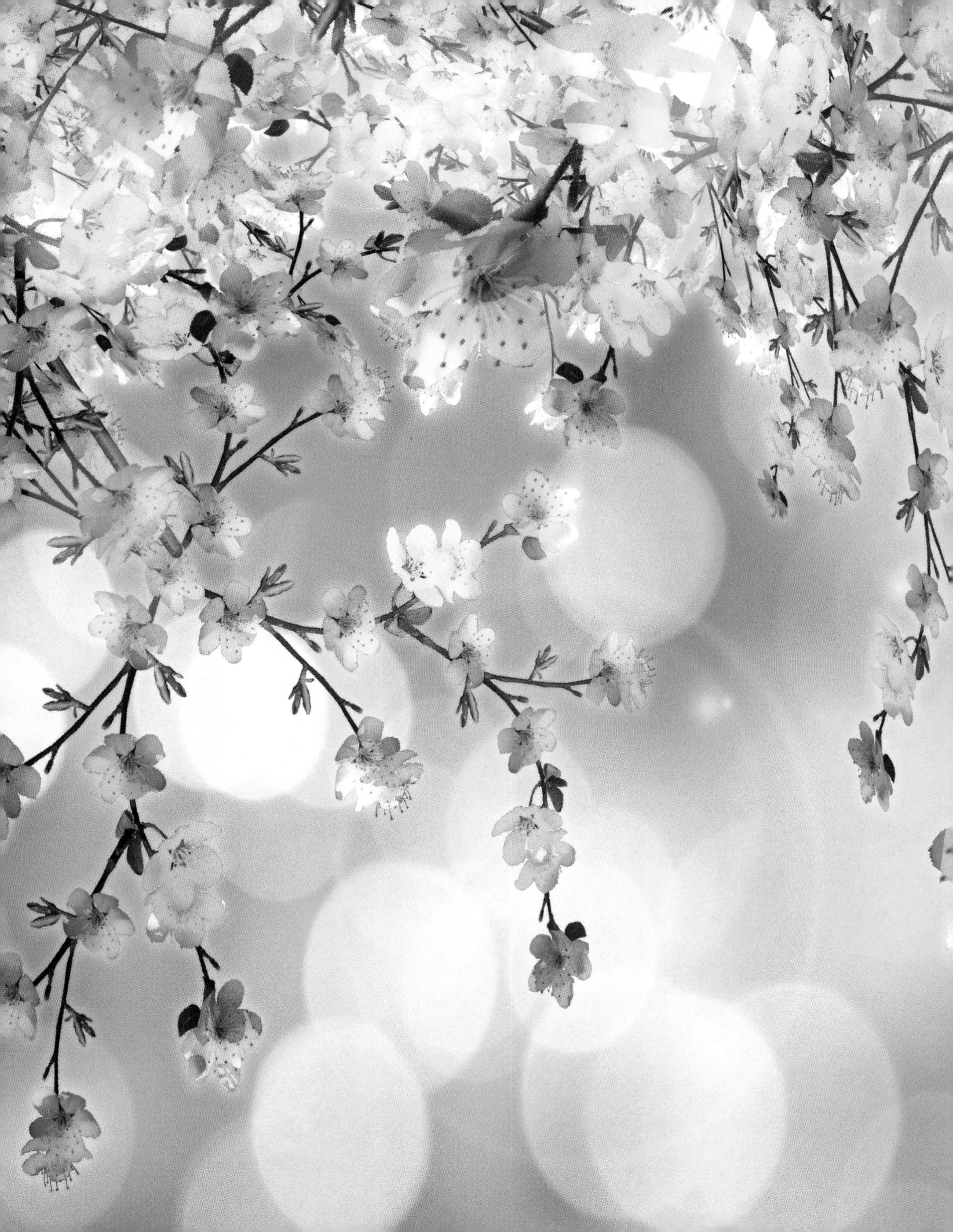

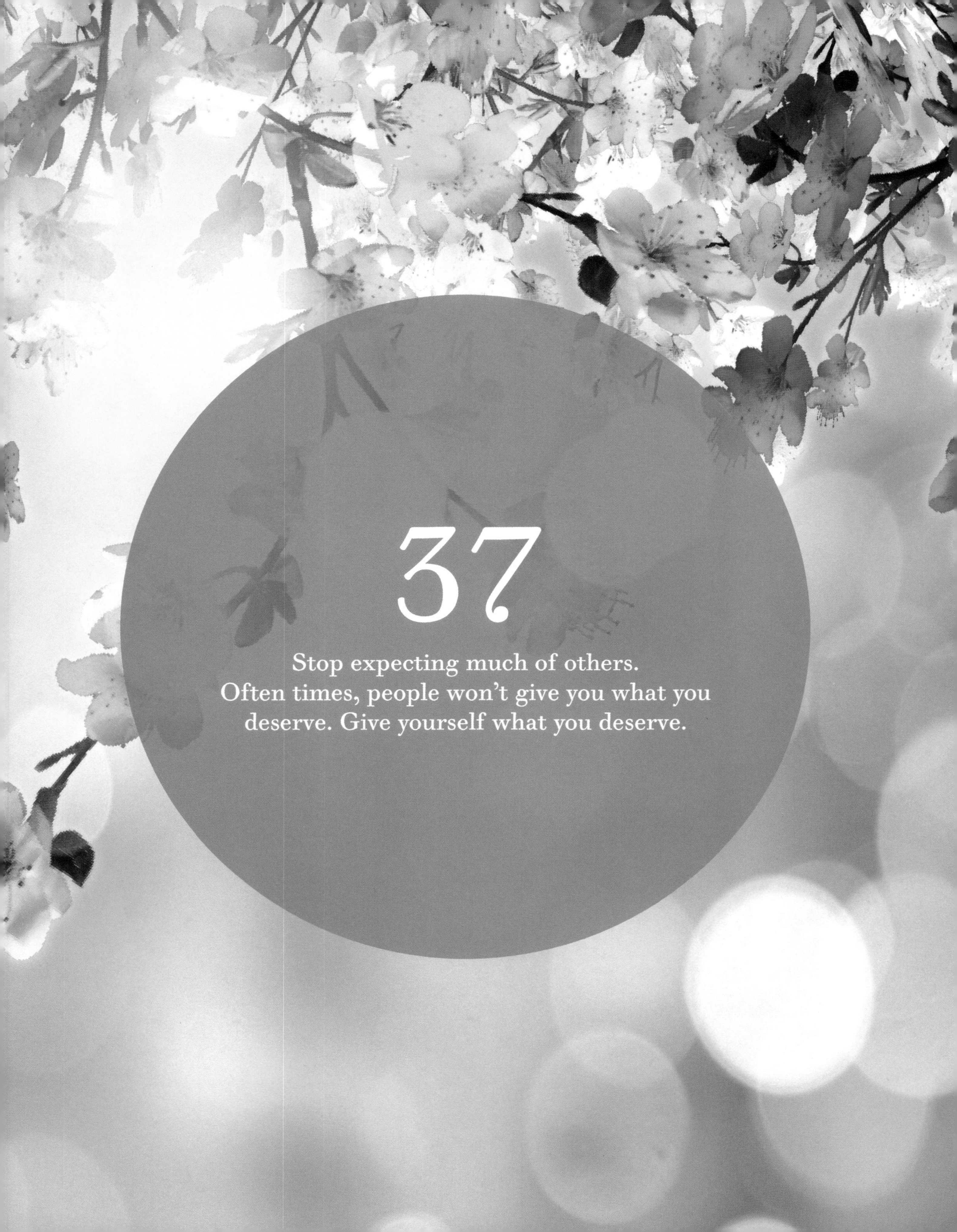

37

Stop expecting much of others.
Often times, people won't give you what you deserve. Give yourself what you deserve.

Date

....

Thought/s:

....

....

....

....

Feeling/s:

....

....

....

....

Behavior/s:

....

....

....

....

Goal/s:

....

....

....

....

Date ....

Notes
....

....

....

....

....

....

....

....

....

....

....

....

....

....

....

....

....

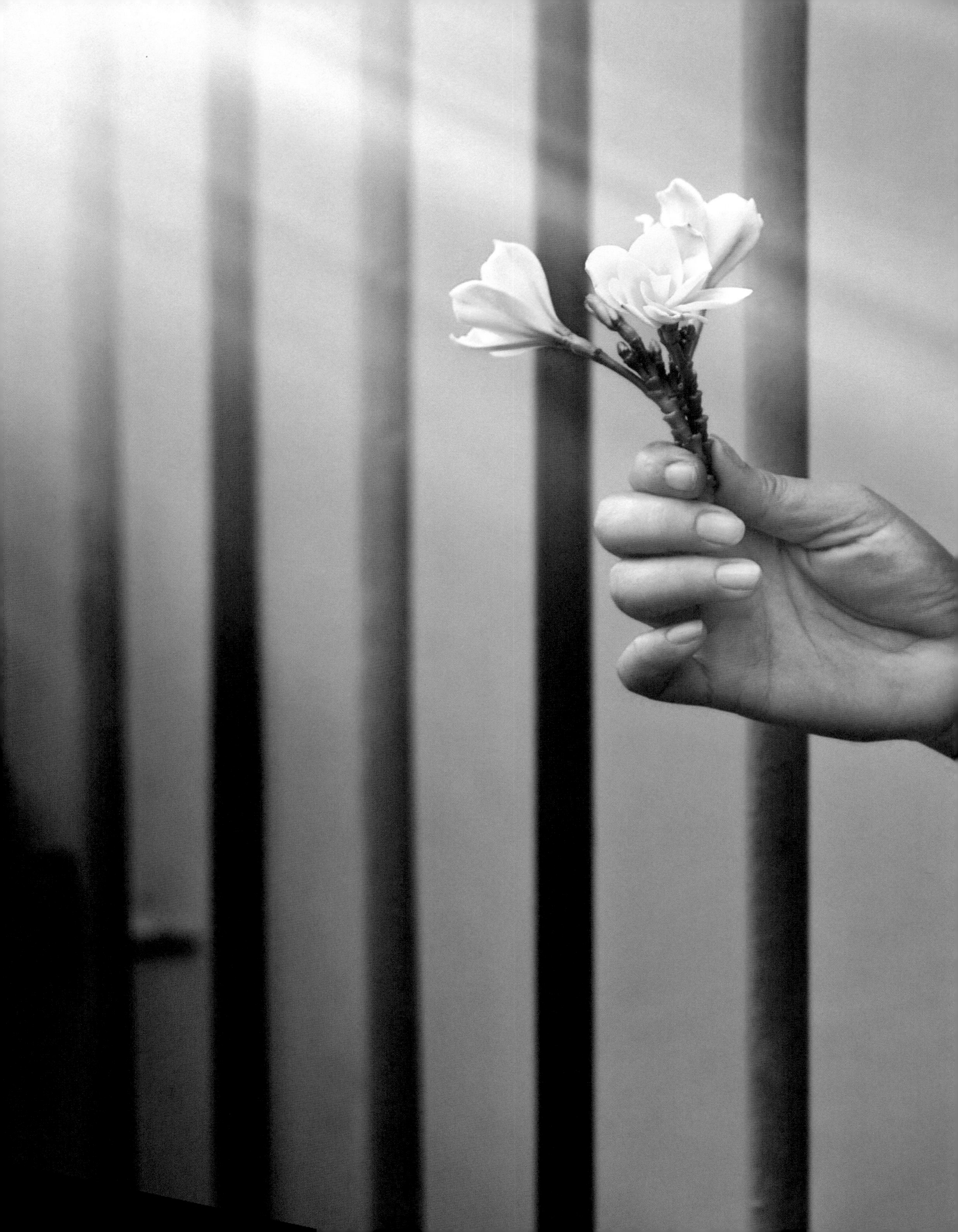

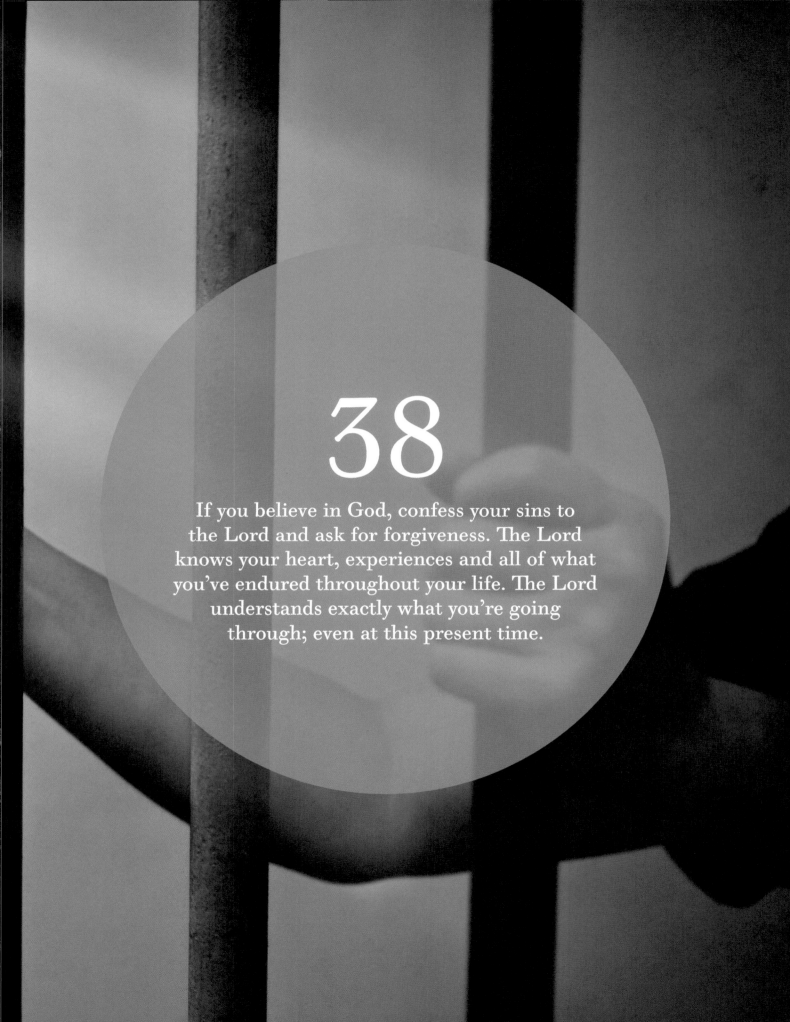

38

If you believe in God, confess your sins to
the Lord and ask for forgiveness. The Lord
knows your heart, experiences and all of what
you've endured throughout your life. The Lord
understands exactly what you're going
through; even at this present time.

Date
....

Thought/s:
....
....
....
....

Feeling/s:
....
....
....
....

Behavior/s:
....
....
....
....

Goal/s:
....
....
....
....

Date

Notes

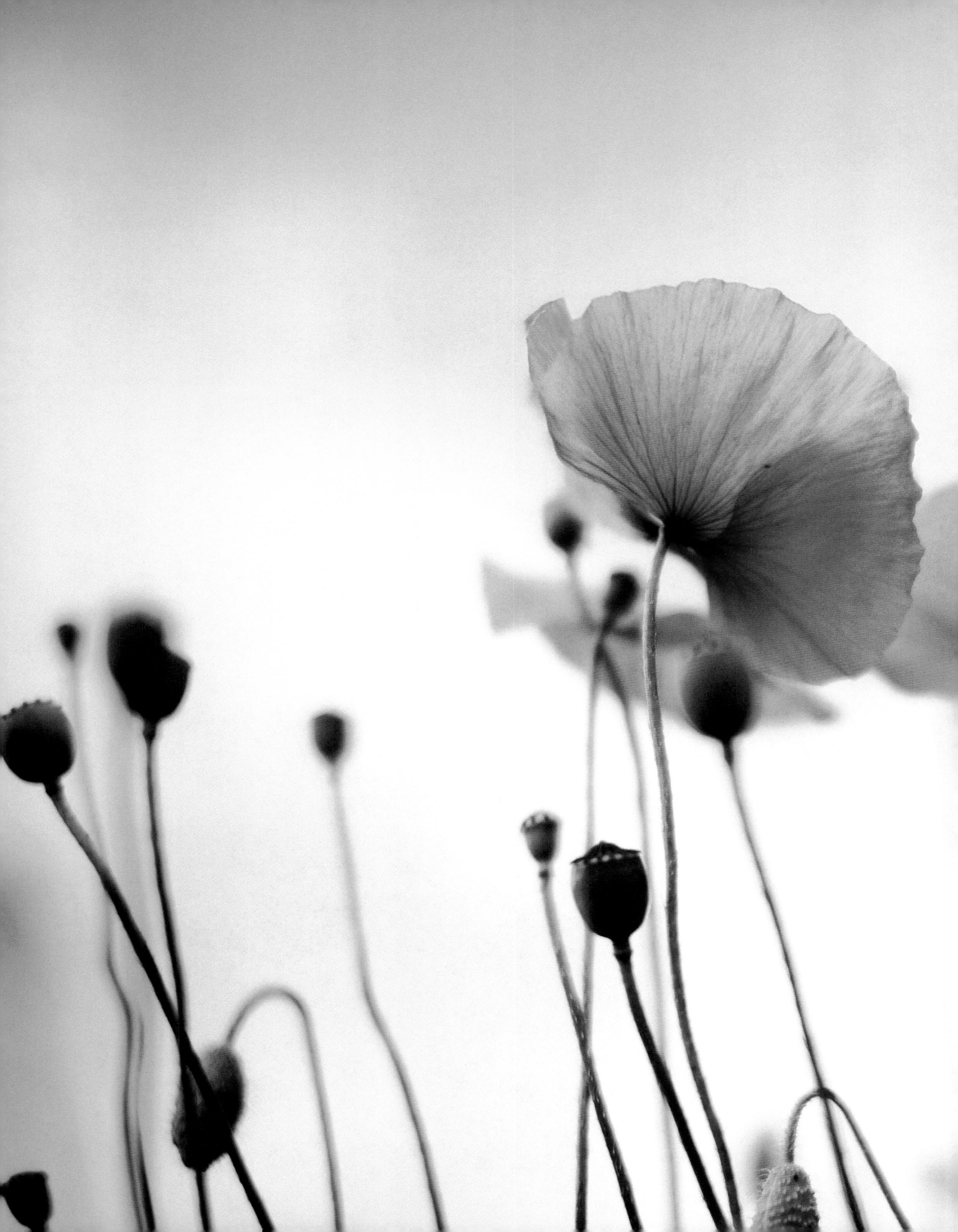

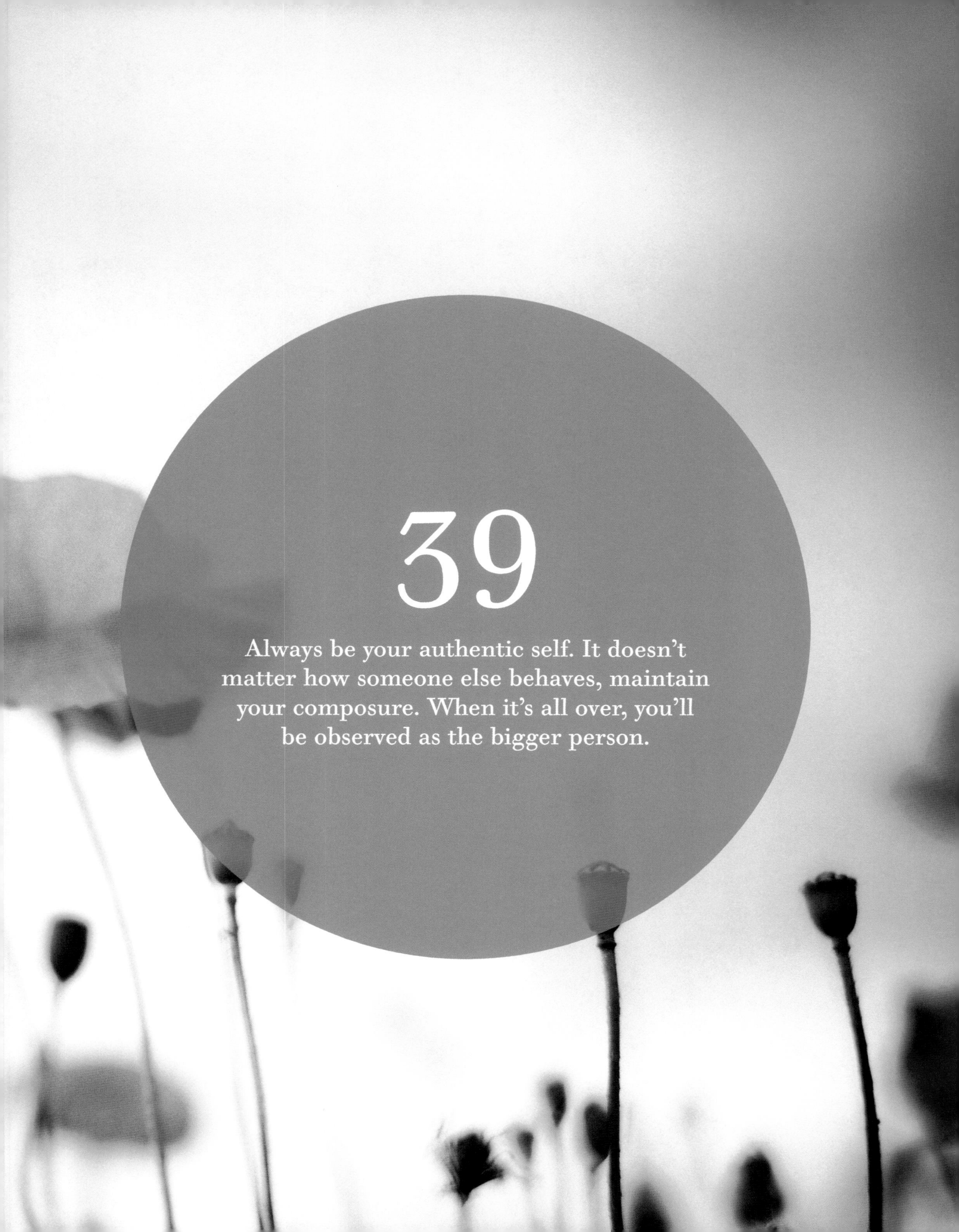

39

Always be your authentic self. It doesn't matter how someone else behaves, maintain your composure. When it's all over, you'll be observed as the bigger person.

Date
....

Thought/s:
....

....

....

Feeling/s:
....

....

....

....

Behavior/s:
....

....

....

....

Goal/s:
....

....

....

....

Date

Notes

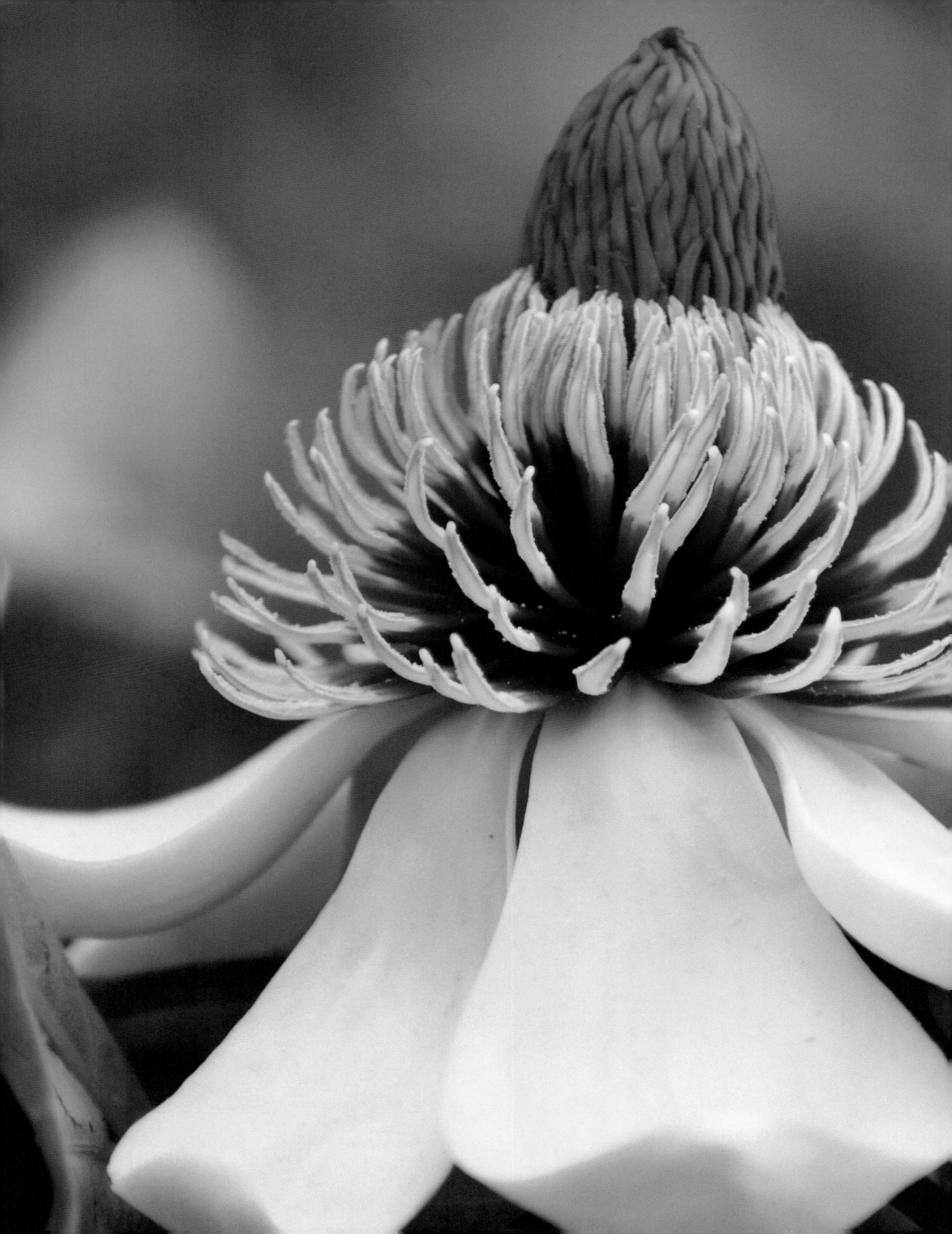

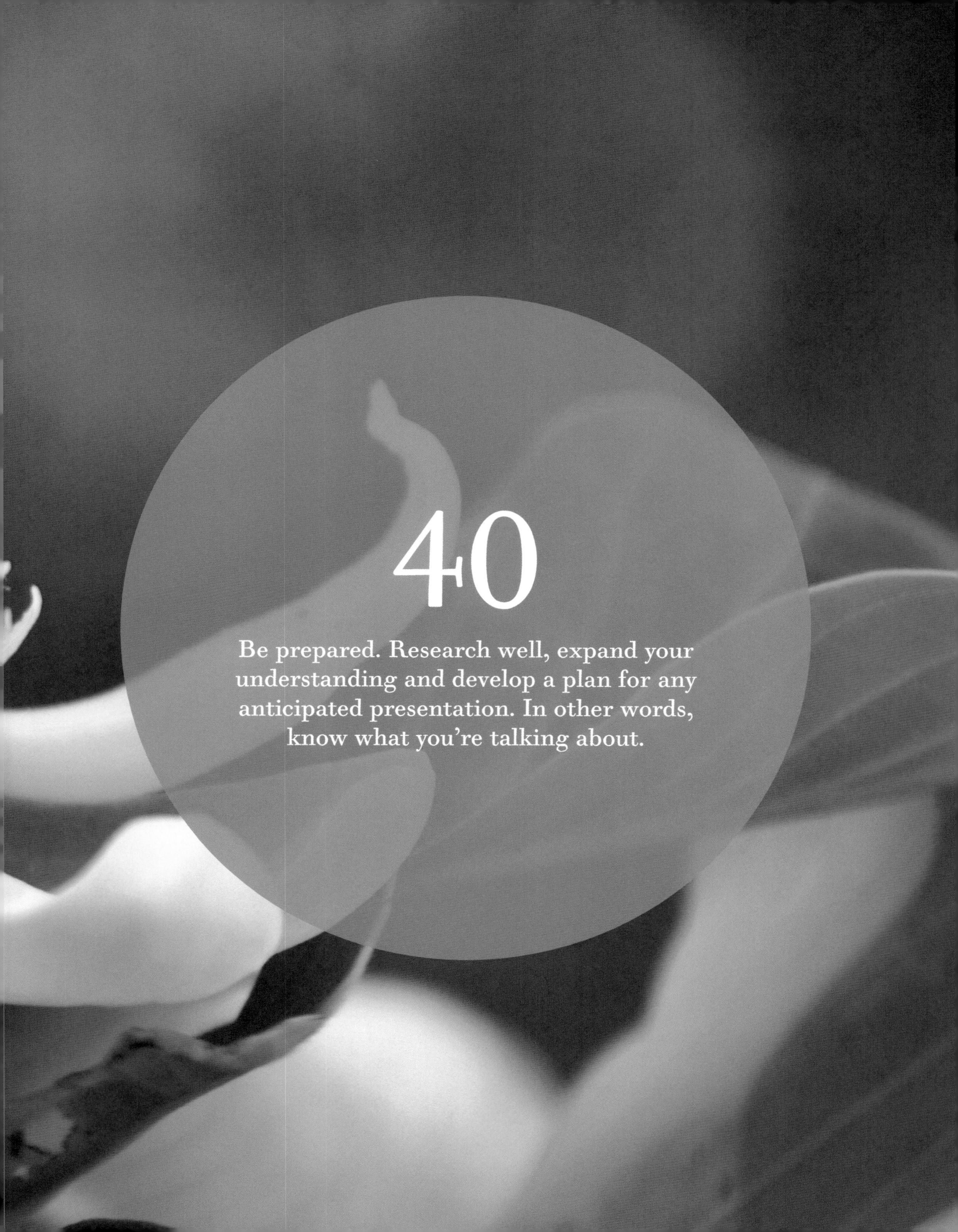

40

Be prepared. Research well, expand your understanding and develop a plan for any anticipated presentation. In other words, know what you're talking about.

Date
....

Thought/s:
....
....
....
....

Feeling/s:
....
....
....
....

Behavior/s:
....
....
....
....

Goal/s:
....
....
....
....

Date

Notes

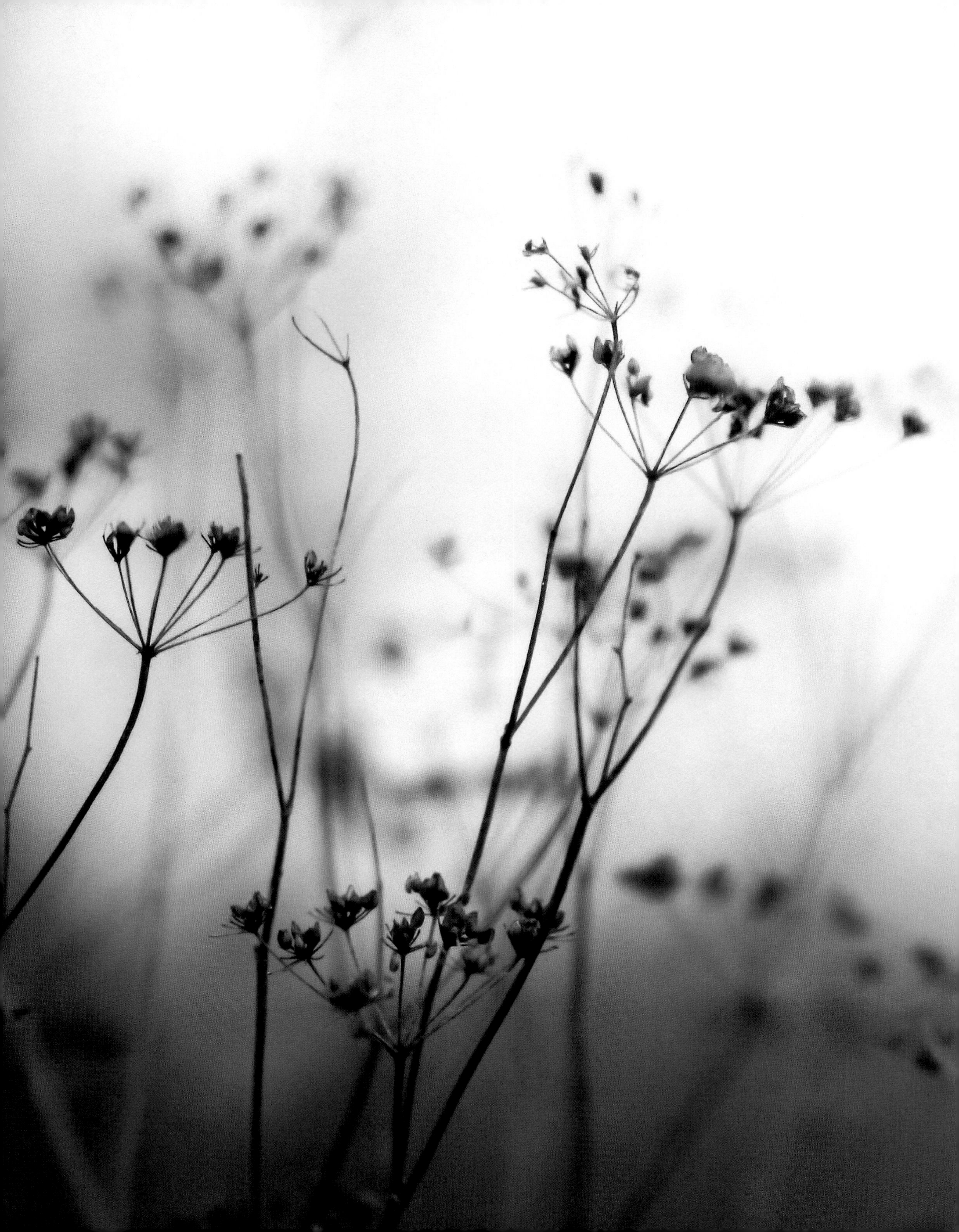

41

Address grief as a chapter that ended, and now, on to the next chapter. Sorrow will last as long as you allow it to. We can't change the past. However, we can restructure our minds.

Thought/s:
....
....
....
....

Feeling/s:
....
....
....
....
....

Behavior/s:
....
....
....
....

Goal/s:
....
....
....
....

Date

Notes

175

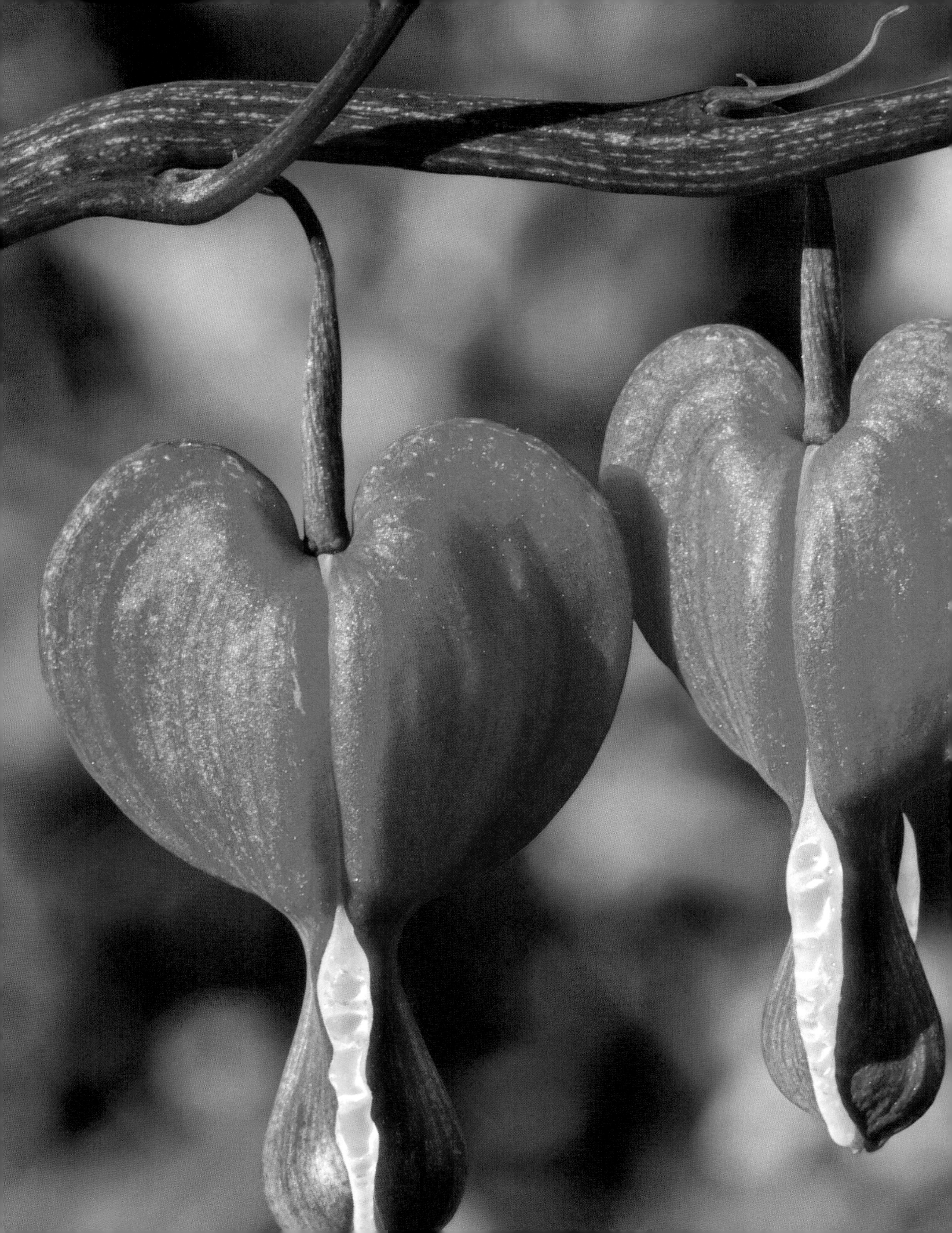

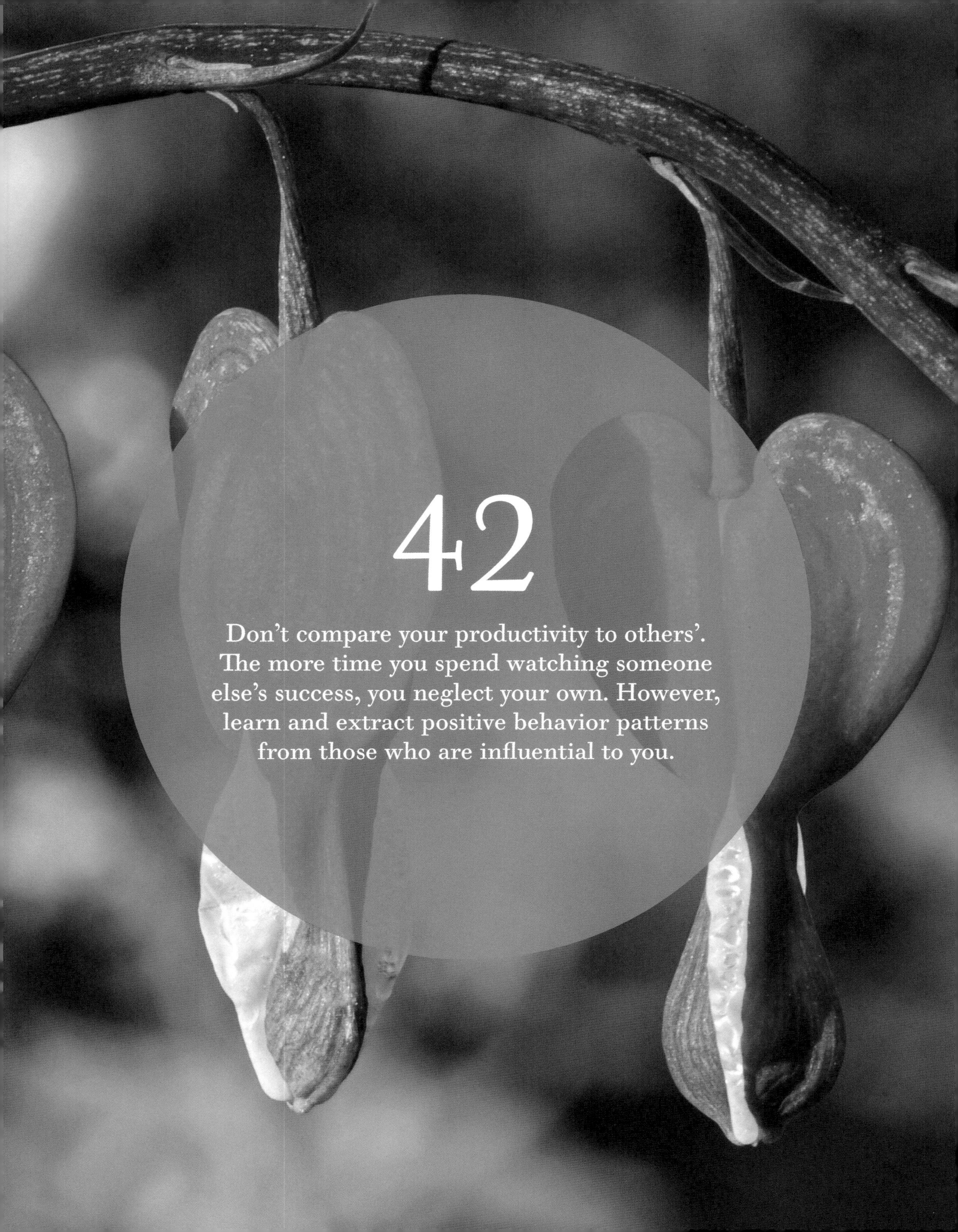

42

Don't compare your productivity to others'. The more time you spend watching someone else's success, you neglect your own. However, learn and extract positive behavior patterns from those who are influential to you.

Date ....

Thought/s:
....
....
....
....

Feeling/s:
....
....
....
....

Behavior/s:
....
....
....
....

Goal/s:
....
....
....
....

Date

Notes

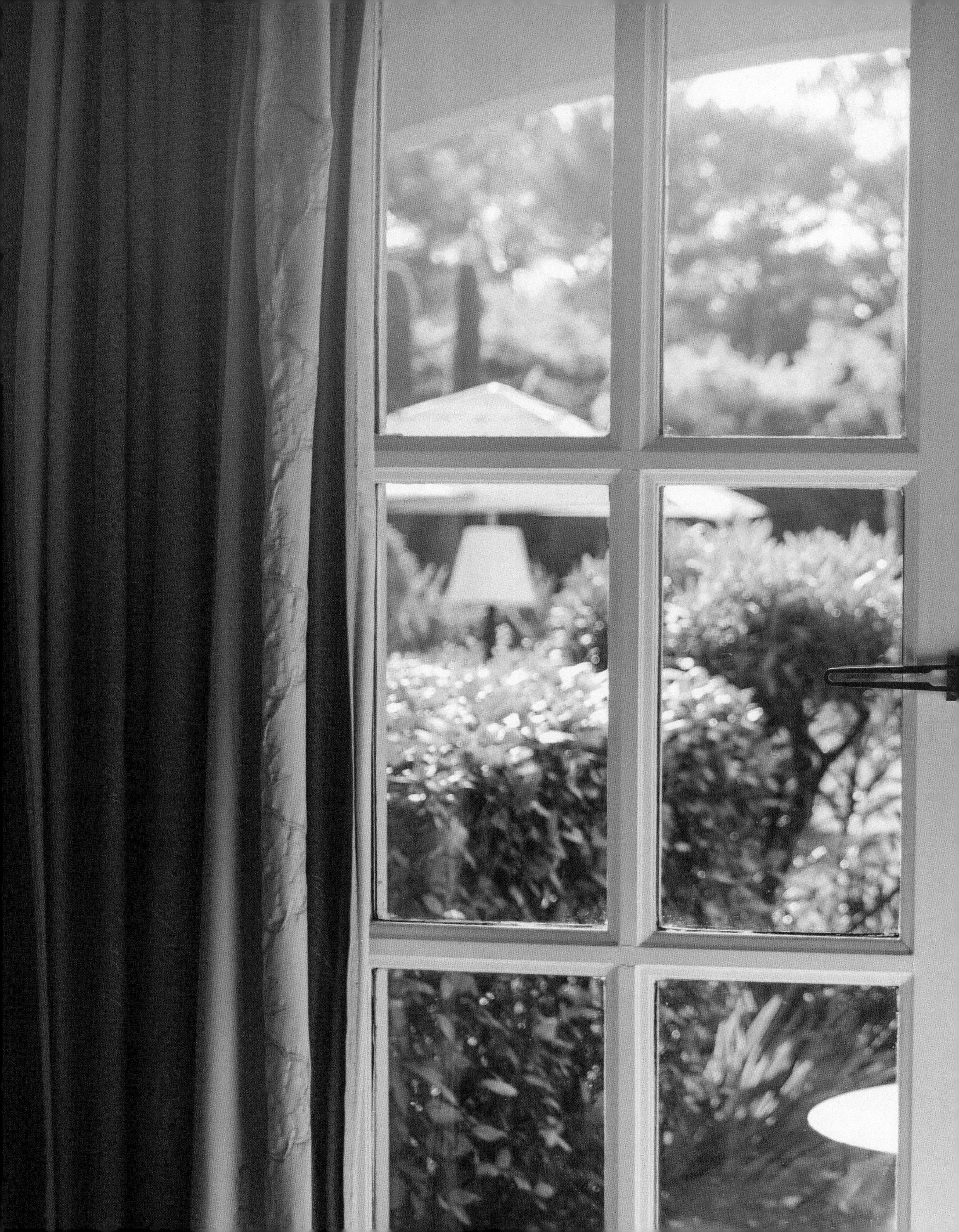

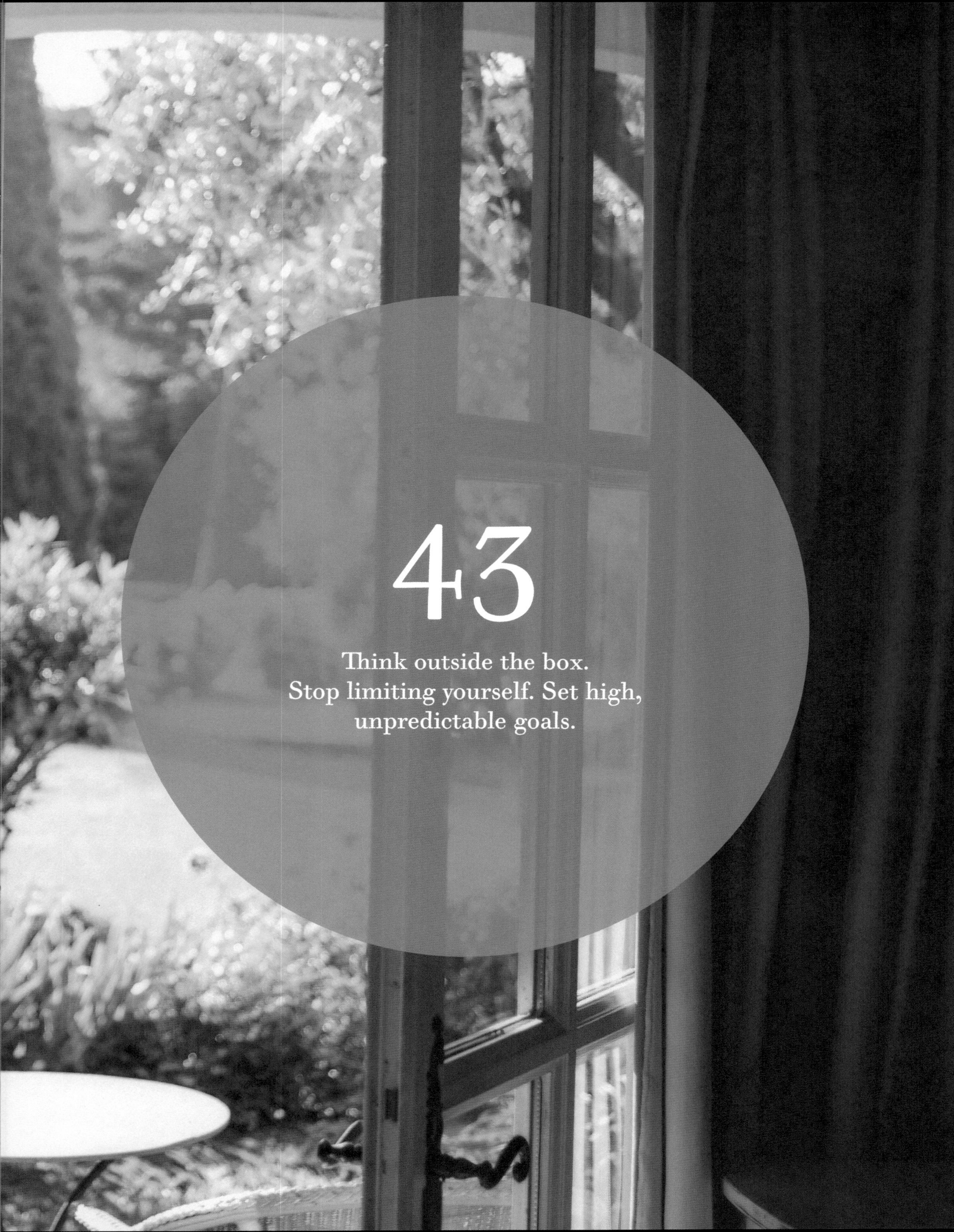

43

Think outside the box.
Stop limiting yourself. Set high,
unpredictable goals.

Thought/s:

....

....

....

....

Feeling/s:

....

....

....

....

Behavior/s:

....

....

....

....

Goal/s:

....

....

....

....

Date
....

Notes
....

....

....

....

....

....

....

....

....

....

....

....

....

....

....

....

....

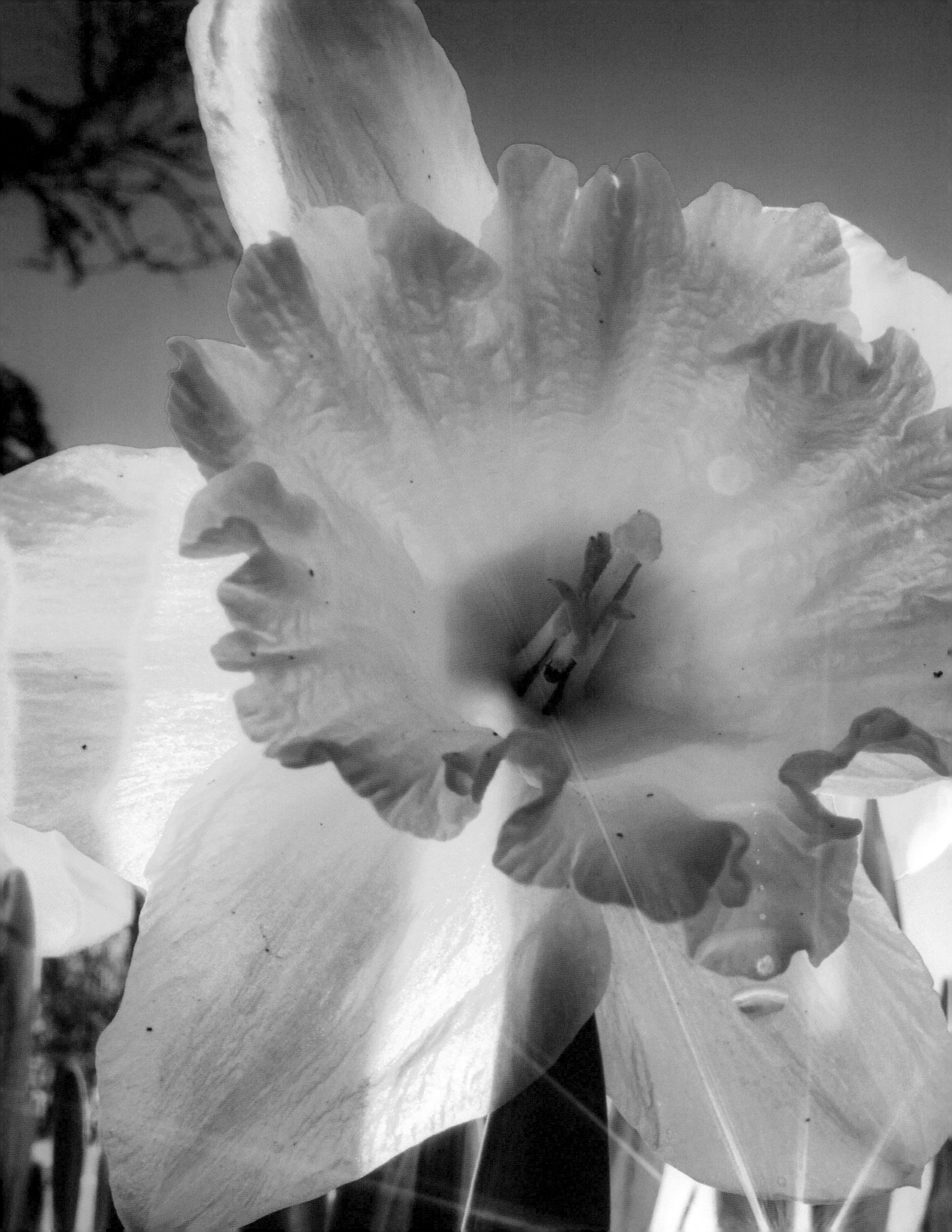

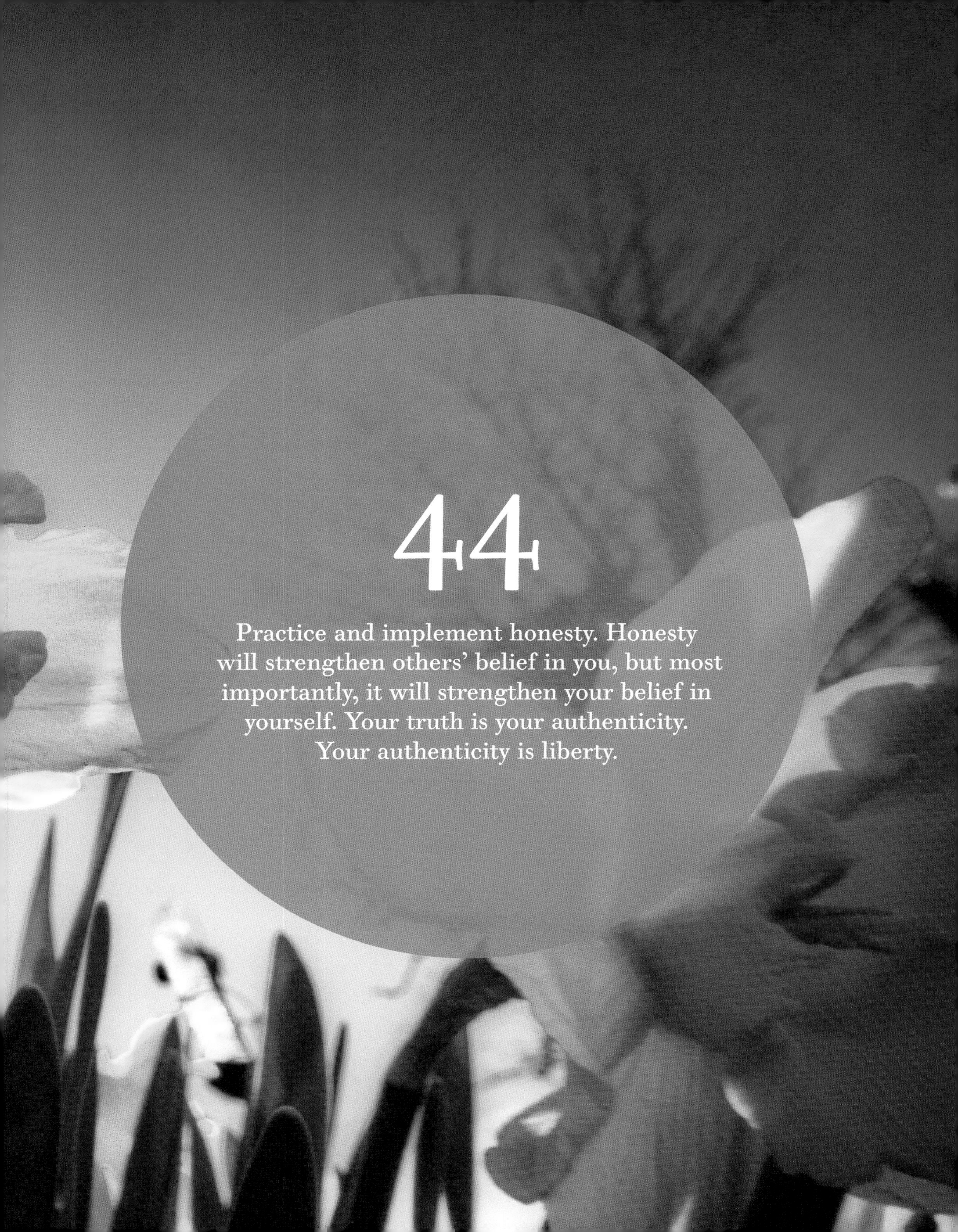

44

Practice and implement honesty. Honesty will strengthen others' belief in you, but most importantly, it will strengthen your belief in yourself. Your truth is your authenticity. Your authenticity is liberty.

Date
....

Thought/s:
....
....
....
....

Feeling/s:
....
....
....
....

Behavior/s:
....
....
....
....

Goal/s:
....
....
....
....

Date ....

Notes
....

....

....

....

....

....

....

....

....

....

....

....

....

....

....

....

....

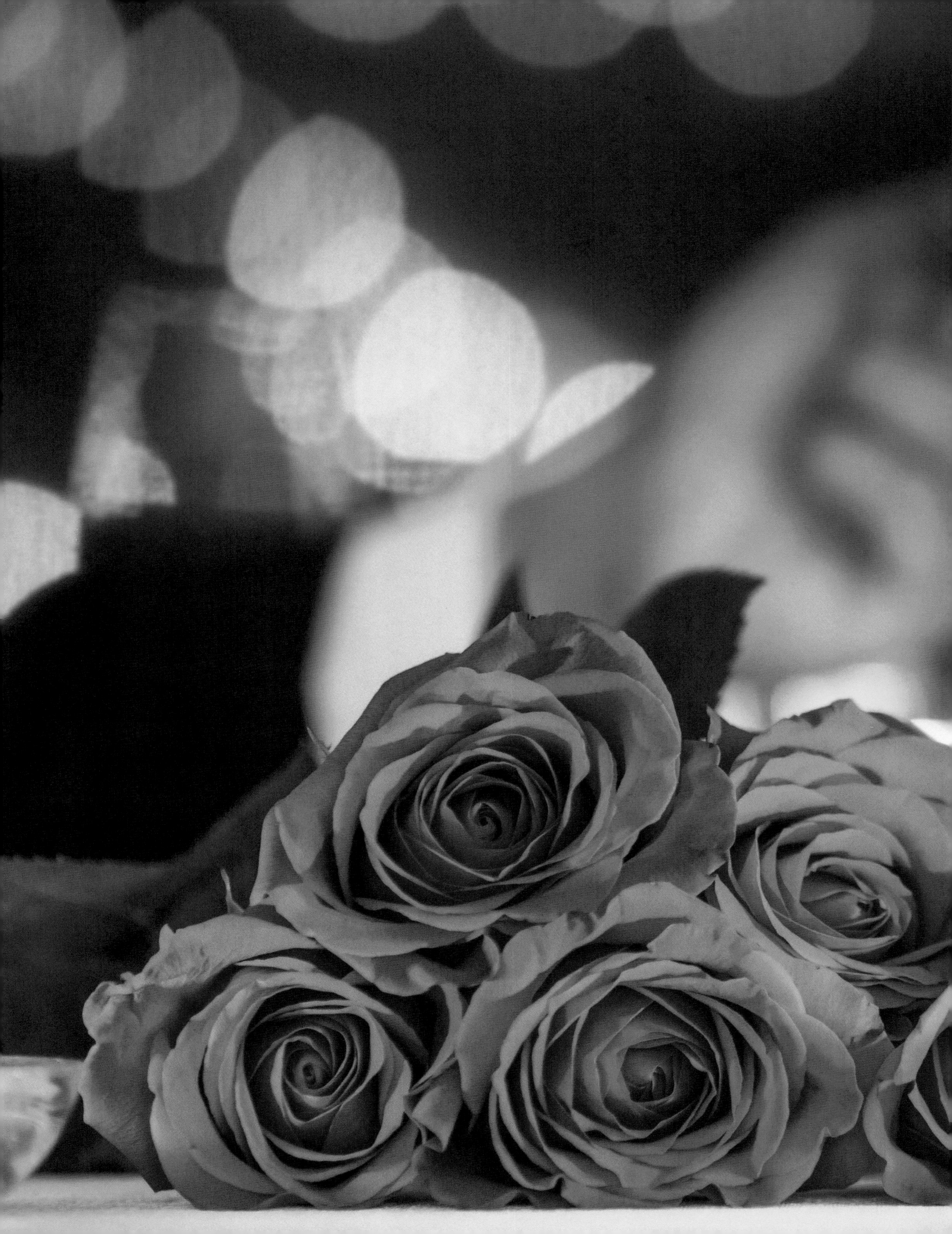

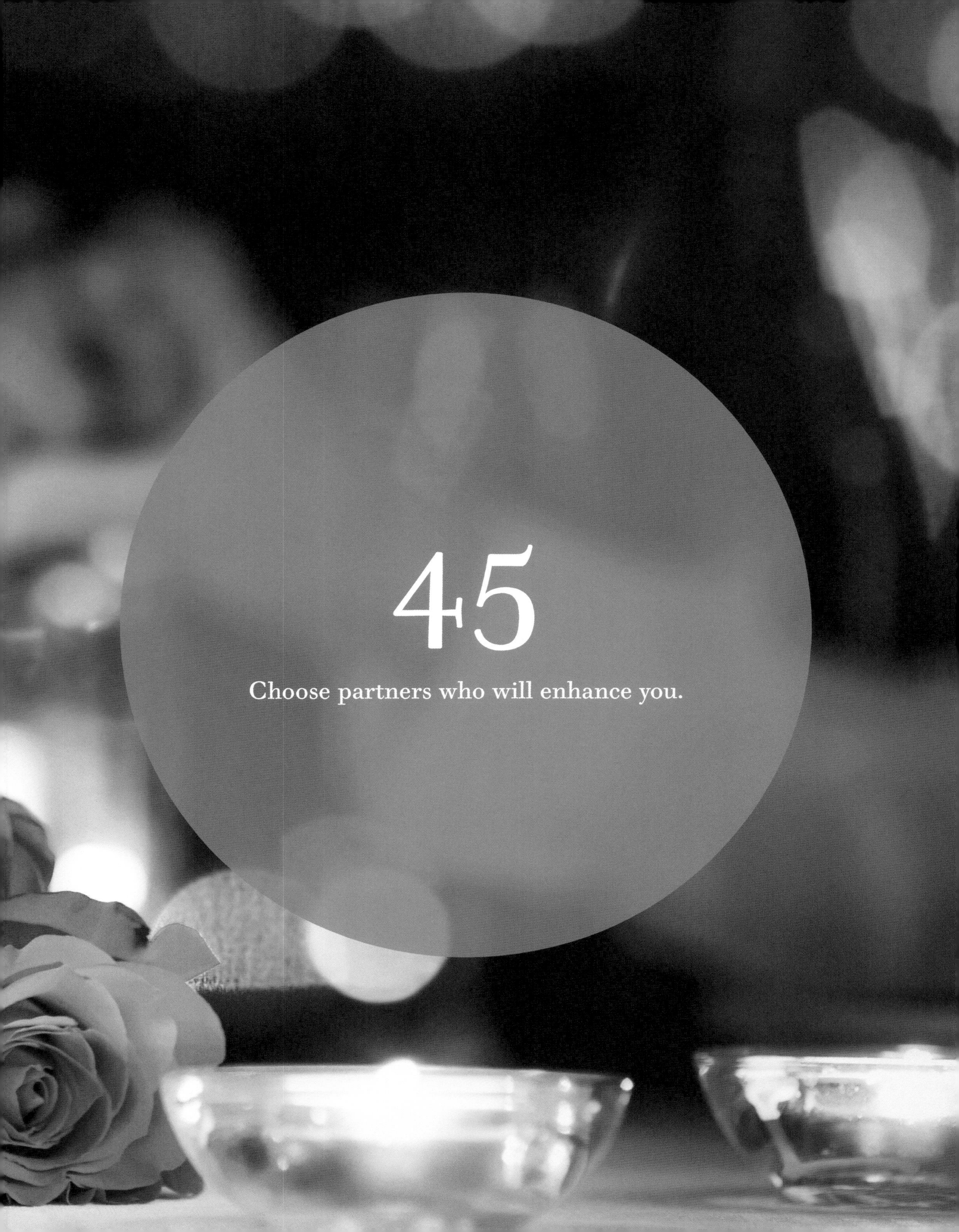

45

Choose partners who will enhance you.

Date
....

Thought/s:
....

....

....

....

Feeling/s:
....

....

....

....

....

Behavior/s:
....

....

....

....

....

Goal/s:
....

....

....

....

Date

Notes

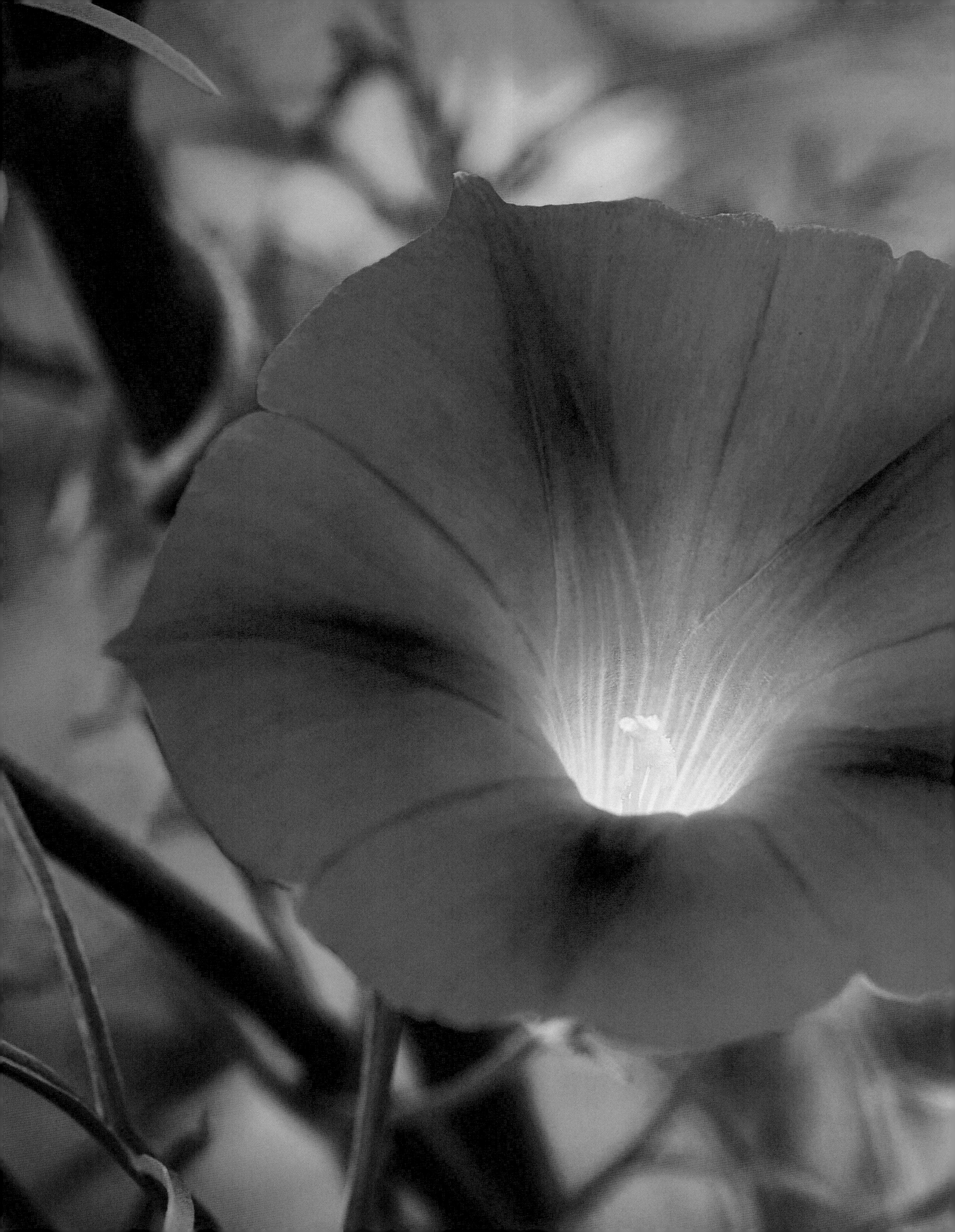

46

Be your best advocate. No one
knows what you want more than you do.
If you're unsure of what you want:

SELF-REFLECT
Consider who you are and what brings you happiness.

RESEARCH
Explore matters that fascinate you.

JOURNAL
Jot down things you like to do.

EDUCATE YOURSELF
Research or take a class on something
that interests you.

THINK OUTSIDE THE BOX
Use your creativity to uncover innovative
ways to expose your skills.

Date
....

Thought/s:
....
....
....
....

Feeling/s:
....
....
....
....
....

Behavior/s:
....
....
....
....

Goal/s:
....
....
....
....

Date ....

Notes
....
....
....
....
....
....
....
....
....
....
....
....
....
....
....
....
....
....

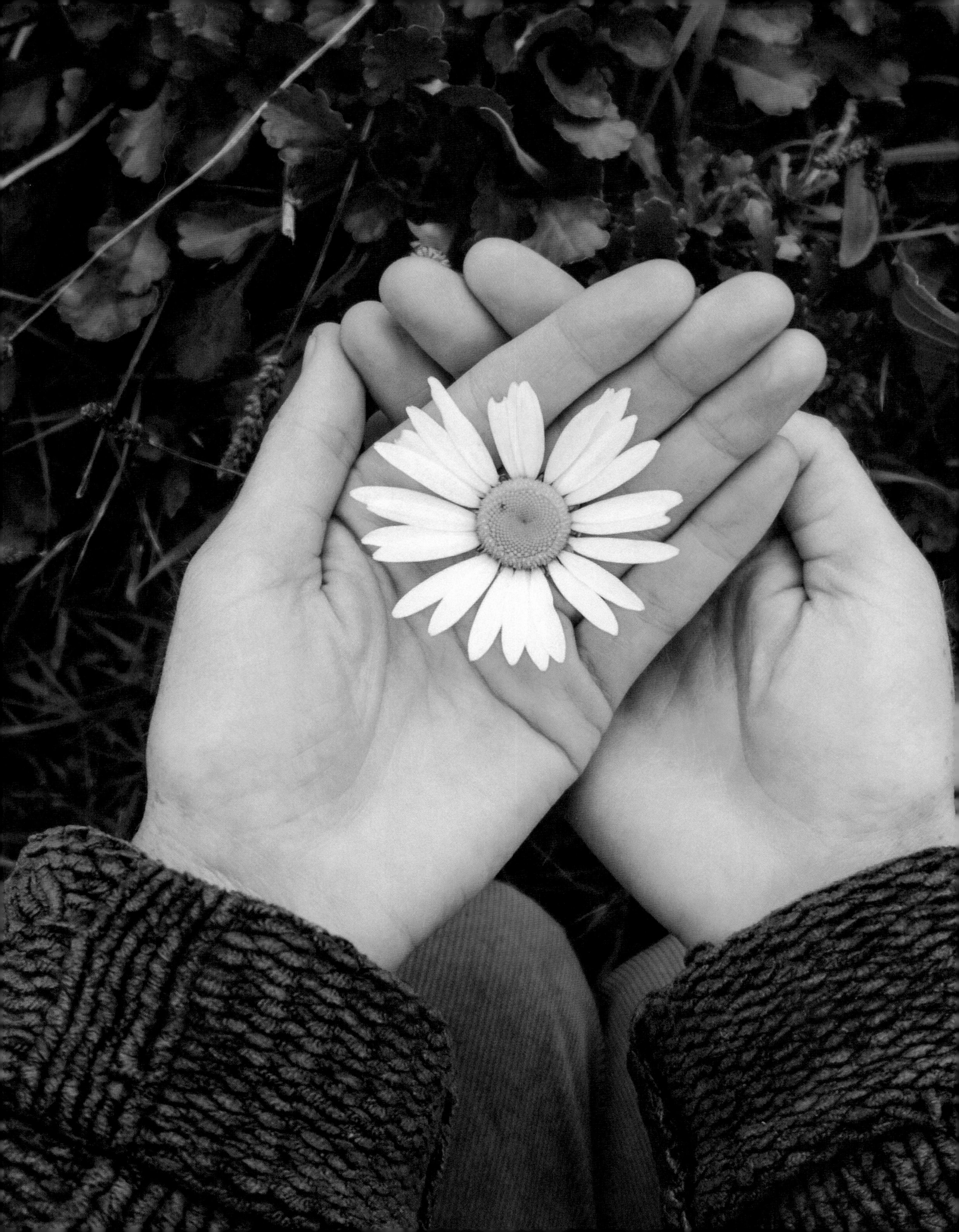

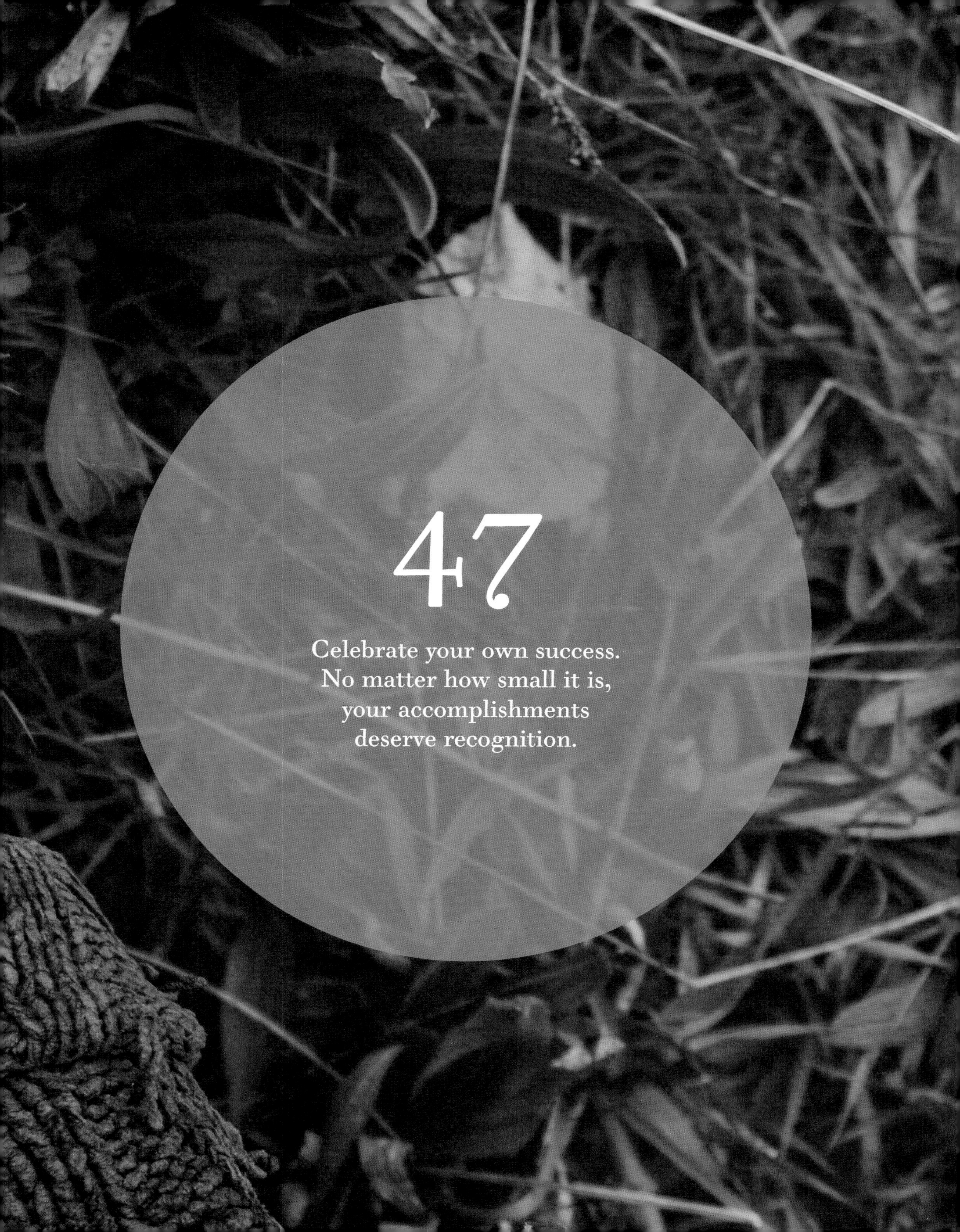

47

Celebrate your own success.
No matter how small it is,
your accomplishments
deserve recognition.

Date
....

Thought/s:
....
....
....
....

Feeling/s:
....
....
....
....

Behavior/s:
....
....
....
....

Goal/s:
....
....
....
....

Date

Notes

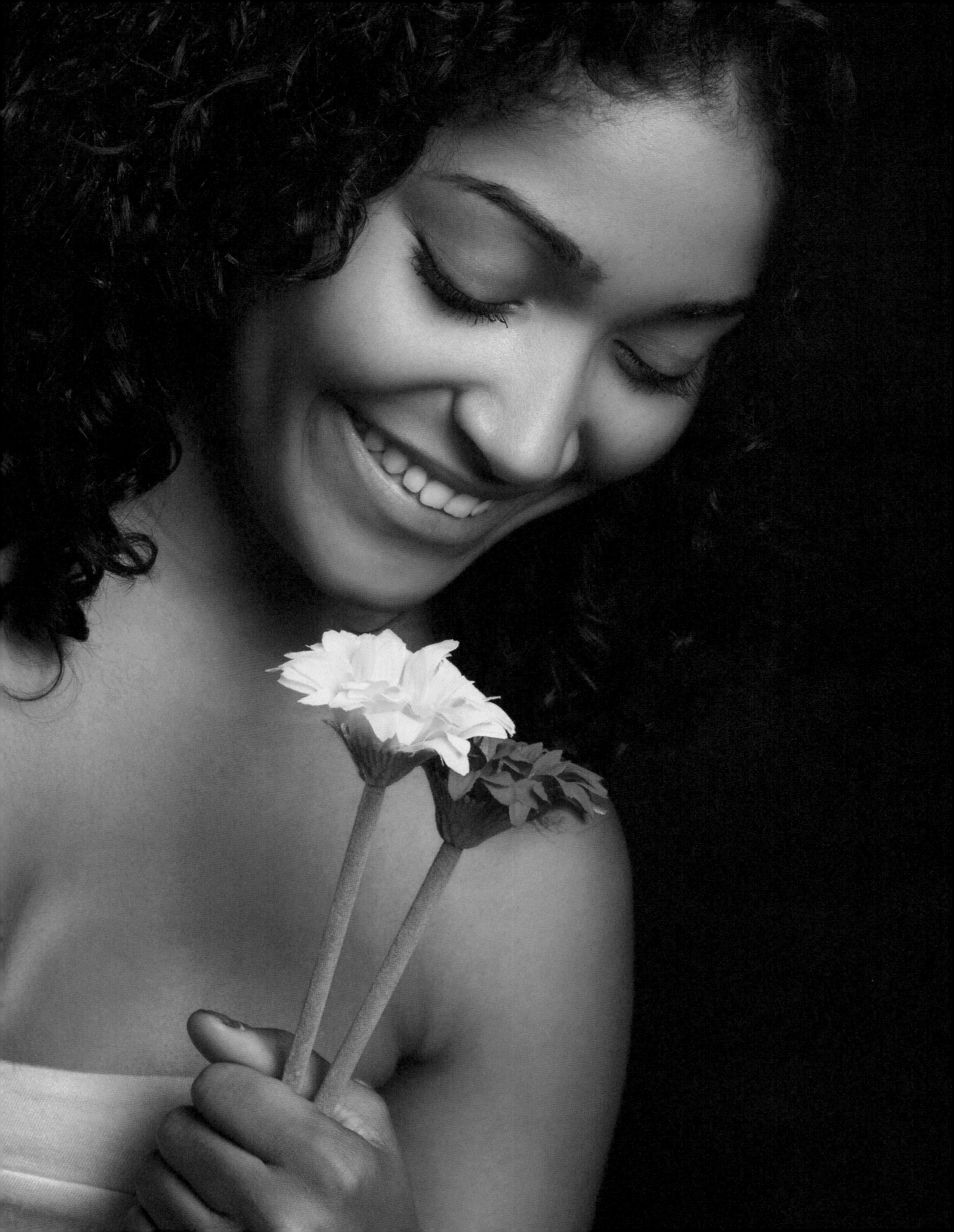

48

Even when it's difficult, smile.
There's always something to
be thankful for.

Date

Thought/s:

Feeling/s:

Behavior/s:

Goal/s:

Date ....

Notes
....
....
....
....
....
....
....
....
....
....
....
....
....
....
....
....
....
....

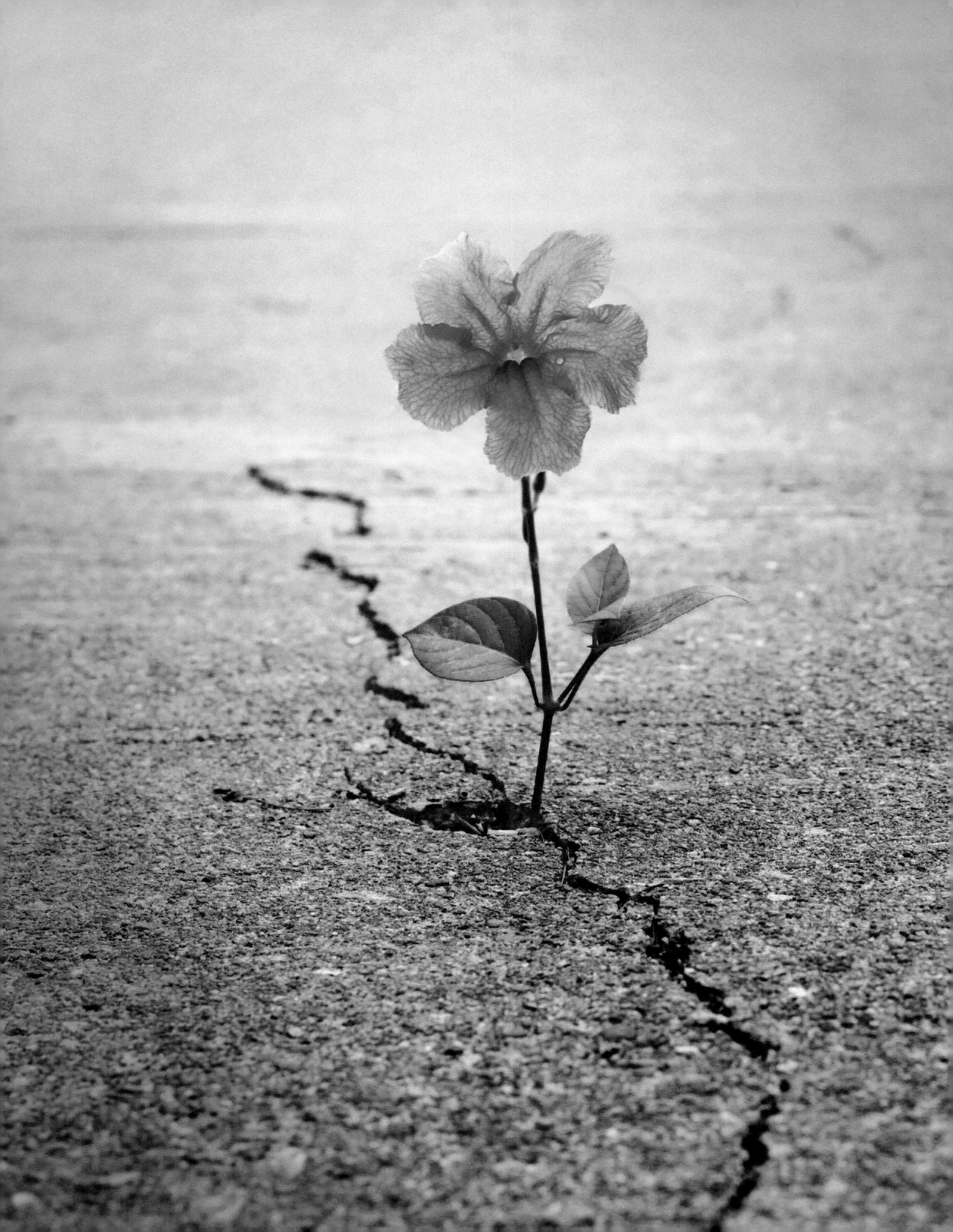

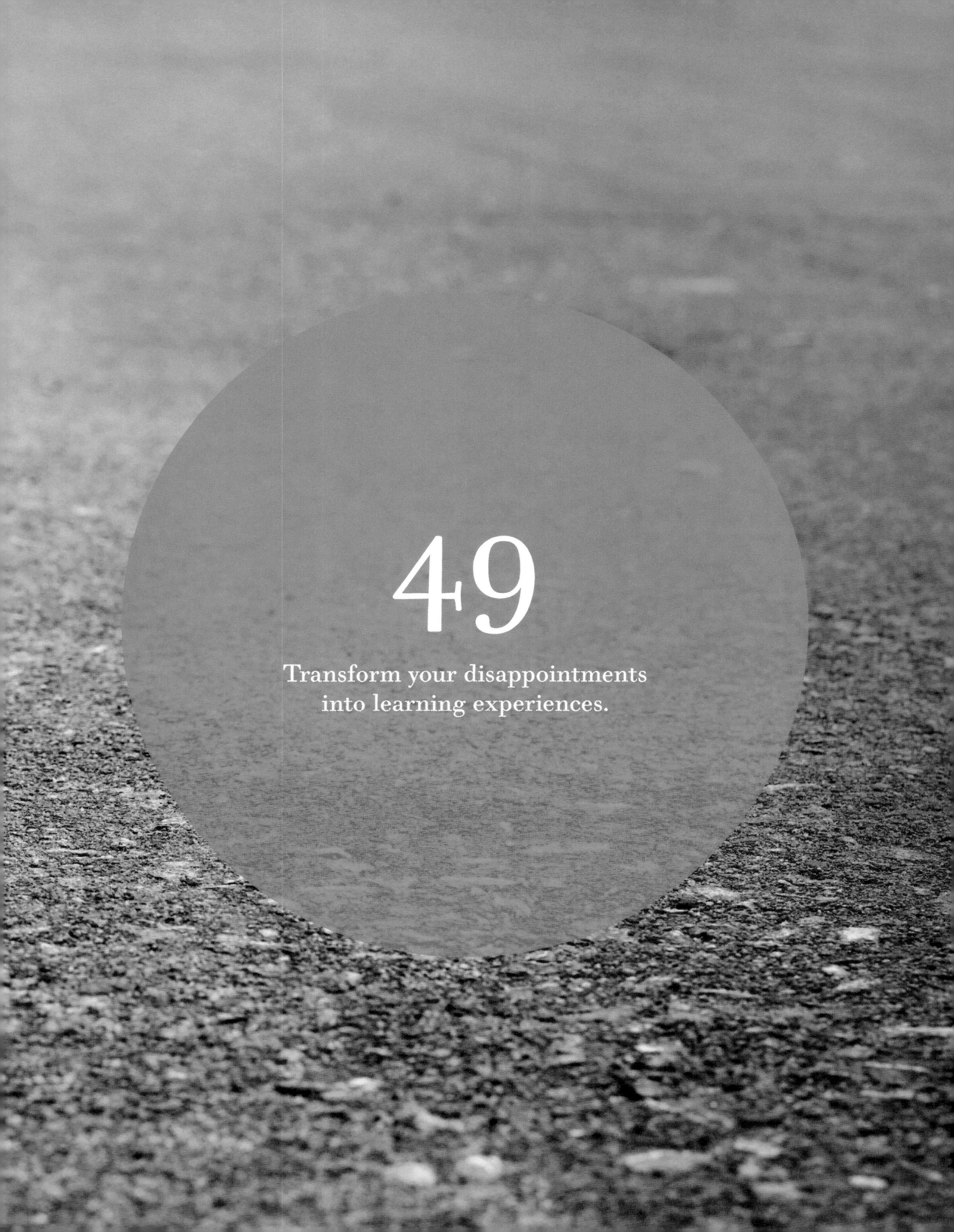

49

Transform your disappointments
into learning experiences.

Date ....

Thought/s:
....
....
....
....

Feeling/s:
....
....
....
....

Behavior/s:
....
....
....
....

Goal/s:
....
....
....
....

Date

Notes

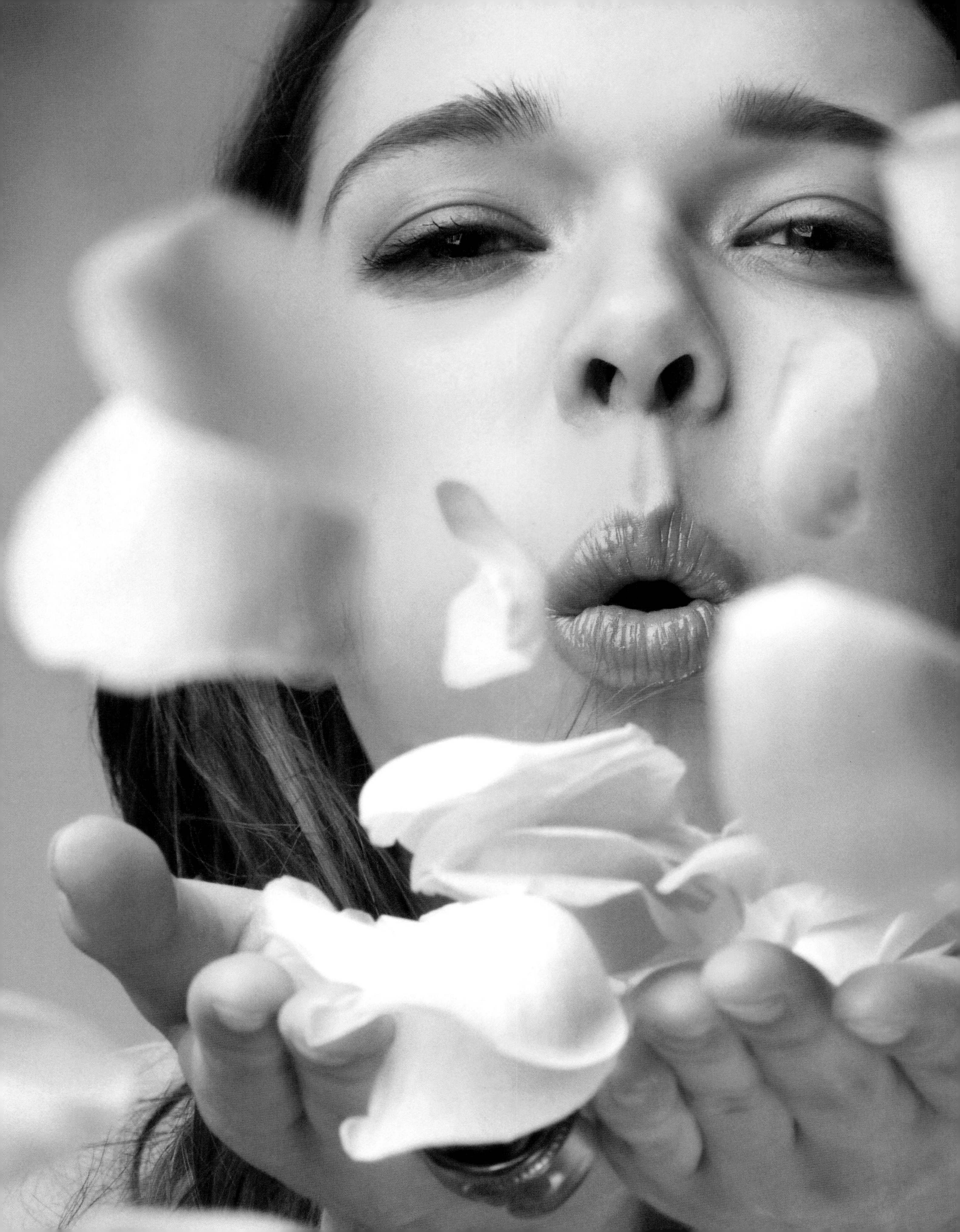

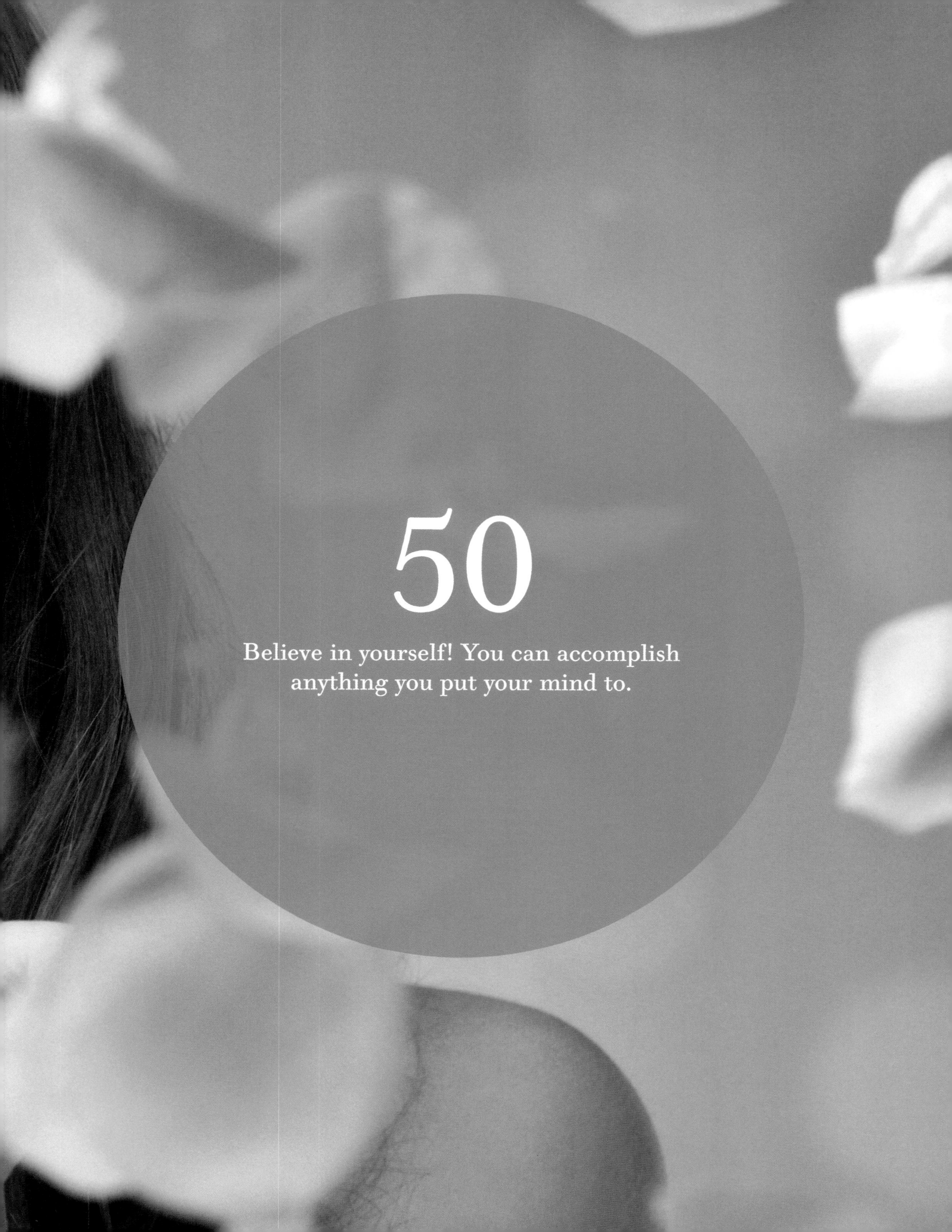

50

Believe in yourself! You can accomplish anything you put your mind to.

Date
....

Thought/s:
....
....
....
....

Feeling/s:
....
....
....
....

Behavior/s:
....
....
....
....

Goal/s:
....
....
....
....

Date

Notes